intranets

Nick Vandome

TEACH YOURSELF BOOKS

Orders: please contact Bookpoint Ltd, 39 Milton Park, Abingdon, Oxon OX14 4TD. Telephone: (44) 01235 400414, Fax: (44) 01235 400454. Lines are open 9.00 – 6.00, Monday to Saturday, with a 24 hour message answering service. E-mail address: orders@bookpoint.co.uk

A catalogue record for this title is available from the British Library.

ISBN 0 340 73789 1

First published 1999
Impression number   10 9 8 7 6 5 4 3 2 1
Year   2004 2003 2002 2001 2000 1999

Typeset by MacDesign, Southampton
Printed in Great Britain for Hodder & Stoughton Educational, a division of Hodder Headline Plc, 338 Euston Road, London NW1 3BH by Cox & Wyman, Reading, Berkshire.

CONTENTS

PREFACE

We have been living with computers for several decades now, yet the computer revolution is still in its infancy. All aspects of our lives are being touched by computers, from shopping to entertainment, and their influence is growing fast. Nowhere is this more pronounced than in the world of business communications. In businesses around the world people are using computers to improve the flow of information around their organisations. At the forefront of this communications crusade are intranets. Intranets are like mini versions of the Internet, operating within organisations, providing information to employees through their desktop computers. Not only are they user-friendly and efficient, they can also save money and cut costs.

The good news about intranets is that you do not have to be a computer expert to either use or create them. A knowledge of working with computers is useful and some general computer experience is recommended if you are going to become involved with your organisation's intranet. However, if you are generally comfortable using a computer then you will be able to design, implement and run an intranet. And if you are nervous about the whole idea of computers and computer networks, then I hope that this book will help to demystify the whole topic.

Although it is not essential to have access to the Internet when you are working with intranets, it is nevertheless very useful. An Internet connection will provide a wide variety of information on intranets and related topics and also allow you to see how various organisations compile their sites. Throughout this book there are references to Internet sites that can be used to find out more about various aspects of using and designing intranets. At the time of writing all of these sites have been checked to make sure that they available and functioning properly. However, due to the nature of the Internet, sites can be discontinued, change location or simply become outdated. If you have any trouble in accessing any of the sites then move on to another one or try searching for a particular topic using one of the Internet search engines, such as Yahoo.

In the world of information technology, the people who bury their heads in the sand in response to new advances are the ones who will be left behind by their more forward-thinking competitors. *Teach Yourself Intranets* is intended to give you the means and the inspiration to stay ahead of the field.

I would welcome any comments or suggestions about the book and I can be contacted at:

nick@vandome.freeserve.co.uk

1 | INTRODUCING INTRANETS

1.1 Defining an intranet

Most people working in an organisation that has any interest in information technology (IT) and innovation will have heard the word 'intranet' being used by both communications and IT staff. In some circles it is the latest buzzword for improved internal communications through the use of computer networks. So what is an intranet? What can it do for organisations? And what can it do for individuals?

In simple terms, an intranet is like a mini version of the Internet. It is a self-contained computer network that can be designed specifically for individual companies or businesses, using the same technology as is employed on the Internet. It is a platform-independent system, which means that it can be operated on a variety of computers and networks. The idea of an intranet is to give everyone in an organisation access to the same information via his or her desktop computers or workstations. This can be anything from telephone directories to annual reports and the beauty of the system is that, once it is up and running, it is immediate, cheap, easy to use and easy to update.

The information on an intranet is held at a central point (a server) and then accessed by individual users via a piece of software called a browser. This allows access to the intranet and then enables the user to 'browse' through the pages that are on it. In general, access to an intranet is limited to those within, or designated by, an organisation and so the security problems inherent with the Internet (access is unlimited and there is the potential for information to be manipulated and misused) are not so acute. In both cases, confidential areas can be protected from unauthorised access, if need be, by the use of firewalls (see Chapter 8 for more on security).

1.2 A bit about the Internet

It is impossible to discuss intranets without a bit of background on their older cousin, the Internet. Development of the Internet began in the 1960s when an American scientist, J.C.R. Licklider, first suggested the possibility of creating linked networks of computers. This was further developed by the Advanced Research Project Agency (ARPA) which created the first genuine computer network, Arpanet, in 1969. Its success encouraged the development of other similar linked networks systems by military and research establishments and universities, mainly in the United States. Though these networks were linked within themselves, there was limited communication between the networks. The main problem was in enabling all of the networked computers to understand the same language. This was overcome in 1973 by the American computer scientists Vinton Cerf and Bob Khan who invented the Transmission Control Protocol/Internet Protocol (TCP/IP) which allowed for different computers to communicate with each other in a common language.

The early days

By the start of the 1980s the academic, research and military networks had joined together to form the basis of the Internet. Initially it was thought that its main role would be as a way of sharing information in the world of education and science. It did this successfully, but it required a fair degree of skill on the part of its users and effort on the part of those who managed its information resources. However, in 1989, an English computer scientist named Timothy Berners-Lee developed the basis for the World Wide Web, with a much simpler means of presenting information, and of linking pages together. The Web has grown at a remarkable rate. Estimates and statistics abound about the number of Internet users and at the end of 1998 the best estimate put the figure at approximately 130 million users in 180 countries, with the majority being in the United States (80 million). Development continues to be very rapid and Internet expansion is currently running at 100 per cent per year. This led Vinton Cerf, at a conference of the Internet Society in Geneva in 1998, to predict that the Internet will be larger than the global telephone system by the middle of the next century. For good measure, he also predicted that one day in the not too distant future we would see the first interplanetary Internet.

Although the Internet and the World Wide Web are often thought of as the same thing they are two very separate entities. The Internet is the collection of computers, modems, telephone lines and servers that are connected to provide the veins through which the information on the system passes. The information is organised in several ways, of which the most important is the World Wide Web. This is a massive collection of millions of pages (or files) that contain anything from news, sport, travel and advertising to games, bulletin boards, and Uncle Bill's Home Page on growing your own tomatoes. Since there is presently virtually no regulation about what can be put on the Internet (there is no overall vetting or editorial control) literally anything can be put on the system, and it is. Anyone who has a connection to the Internet (via a personal computer or an Apple Mac, a modem and a link via an Internet Service Provider) can create their own page and put it on the World Wide Web for all to see. Like intranets, the Internet is viewed through a browser. These are provided free of charge and the two most widely used are Netscape Navigator and Microsoft Internet Explorer.

1.3 Defining identities

The key similarity between the Internet and an intranet is the technology they use, in terms of both hardware and software. However, this is where the common ground ends.

The Internet is a sprawling, uncontrolled creation that is still trying to establish its true identity; is it a business tool, a leisure pastime, or just a toy for those obsessed by new computer technology? Because of its size, it is hard to say how the Internet will develop in the future, but it is possible that at least part of it will become increasingly used for business purposes such as research, electronic commerce (e-commerce) and administrative tasks. However, only time will tell.

By contrast, an intranet is a controlled and focused system that is very sure of its identity: it is a specific business tool that should be used as such. Everything that is put on it should serve a business purpose and there is no room for showing off or for computer one-up-manship. Intranets and the Internet may come from the same family background but they both have very different personalities.

1.4 LANs and WANs

As with most things connected with computers, there is a certain amount
of jargon associated with intranets. Two common terms that will occur
when intranets are being discussed are Local Area Networks (LANs) and
Wide Area Networks (WANs). These are phrases that describe a particular
type of computer network. In simple terms, a LAN is a collection of
computers that are connected together so that they can share a wide range
of electronic information. They generally operate over relatively short
distances, within a single office or covering a range of a few kilometres,
and they are an efficient and cost-effective way of sharing information
and data. WANs are similar to LANs except that they connect computer
networks over larger distances. It is possible to connect separate LANs
together and also to connect them to WANs, through the use of devices
called gateways, routers and bridges.

Local Area Networks and Wide Area Networks are obviously of great
interest to anyone thinking of creating an intranet. For the system to be
able to operate in the first place it needs to have in place a LAN or a WAN
so that the information on the intranet can be accessed by all of the relevant
users. For a local or small intranet a LAN is sufficient, but for a larger
one, that may stretch between countries, a WAN must be in place. There
are a number of major IT companies that specialise in establishing LANs
and WANs including Novell, IBM, Microsoft and Hewlett Packard. More
information on networks can be obtained from their respective Internet
sites at:

> http://www.novell.com/
>
> http://www.ibm.com/
>
> http://www.microsoft.com/
>
> http://www.hewlett-packard.com/

Internet addresses are known as Uniform Resource Locators (URLs) and
these are dealt with in more detail in Chapter 3, page 41.

1.5 Who can benefit?

An intranet is a business tool and offers huge potential to large areas of
the business community, including organisations such as universities,
schools, the public sector and charitable bodies. Obviously, this does not

cover every single business or organisation – a self-employed tradesman or a family-run small business may not have much need for an intranet. But for any company with over 100 employees, intranets can offer significant benefits in terms of:

- Cost-savings
- Time-savings
- Improved communications
- Improved overall morale

The size of the organisation will determine the best type of intranet for the circumstances:

Small organisations (100—300 employees)

For a small business, a fairly basic, simple intranet would be ideal. It could contain important information such as client details, product details and personnel information. It should aim to inform the staff without including too much additional information that they do not really need.

Medium organisations (300–1,000 employees)

For medium businesses the intranet really begins to come into its own. Different sections can create their own pages so that everyone in the organisation knows what everyone else is doing; training opportunities can be publicised; staff moves can be indicated immediately, and it is an ideal way to link employees in different geographical locations.

Large organisation (over 1,000 employees)

The larger the organisation, then the greater the potential benefits from an intranet. The cost savings increase with a greater number of users and several other functions can also be performed: booking meeting rooms, sharing research; linking people in different locations and conducting on-line training.

Multinationals (over 1,000 employees, operating in more that one country)

For a company of this size an intranet will be a true international operation. It will have input from dozens, or hundreds, of people and it will need careful control to make sure it serves its purpose in all of the countries in which it operates.

1.6 Transforming your organisation

The first thing to realise about an intranet is that it is not an IT toy or a
new piece of computing gimmickry, despite what the IT people might
say. Neither is it a communications device that will automatically and
instantly improve the way you operate. It is a powerful communications
tool that has the potential to transform your business in a variety of ways
but it needs careful planning, installation and maintenance for it to succeed.
If you take the views of IT and communications staff and then look at the
middle ground then you may get a realistic vision of the intranet.

Despite some claims to the contrary, intranets are not usually installed
and running within a matter of days – 18 months is a more realistic
timescale. The reason for this is undoubtedly the human factor. Although
the hardware (the network) and the software (the server and browsers)
required to run the intranet can be installed quickly, the human element
does not always keep up with this. From the moment a decision is taken
to look at an intranet a number of hurdles need to be overcome:

- Managing directors must be convinced that it will be effective.
- Financial directors need to be reassured that it will bring
  genuine financial benefits.
- Editorial control needs to be established (usually a debate
  between IT and communications staff, which should **always**
  be won by the latter).
- Staff have to be consulted.
- Some pages for the intranet need to be created.
- The system needs to be given a trial.
- Staff need to be won over to the final product.

So the setting up of an intranet is not an instantaneous process, if you
want it to succeed. Planning, consultation and attention to detail are
essential for an effective intranet and if this is done then the final product
really will have the potential to transform the way your organisation
operates.

1.7 Identifying the benefits

Once a well planned and maintained intranet is up and running, some benefits will be immediately obvious. The key words here are 'well planned' and 'maintained'. Although at first sight an intranet may seem like something that can be thrown together and implemented relatively quickly this is not the best approach. If you really want the intranet to benefit your organisation then some time and effort should be put into producing it properly. This is discussed in greater detail in Chapter 2. However, if an intranet is produced and implemented with care and consideration then you will soon notice a difference.

Less paper

The first benefit you should see from the intranet is that the piles of papers that lie around your office are dramatically reduced (not completely eliminated though, as the idea of a paperless office seems to be something of an office manager's utopia). Instead of having telephone directories, memos, notices, directories and reports lying around on desks and in filing cabinets, all of this information can now be on the intranet. This brings immediate tangible benefits: reduced paper costs; reduced printing costs; reduced distribution costs; and reduced storage costs. Many companies are already experiencing these benefits. A firm of London stockbrokers is currently saving 3,000 tonnes of paper a year through the use of their intranet and British Telecom (BT), who run Europe's largest intranet, estimate to have saved £600 million, mainly on the costs associated with producing and distributing printed documents.

If you do get rid of a lot of your paper-based documents and the system then crashes, you will need to have a procedure in place to handle this (see Chapter 6, page 91). Equally, the users have to know what to do if the system crashes: let them know what will happen and also issue them with a hotline telephone number to call in the event of system failure.

Up-to-date information

The second benefit from an intranet is that information can be updated quickly and easily. This means that time is not wasted trying to find the telephone extension of people who have moved or the wrong product information is given out because the directory has not been updated. This ensures that staff are able to do their jobs more quickly and they are also better informed. This not only improves customer service; it also boosts staff morale because people feel they can get on more effectively with their job.

Better communications

The third advantage of an intranet is that the workforce has a better understanding of what happens in the rest of the organisation. This is particularly relevant if the company is located in more than one geographical location. Instead of feeling dissociated from the 'centre' of the company, all of the workforce can be linked together on an equal footing via the intranet. If someone in a personnel division wants to know what their marketing department is doing they only have to check the relevant information on the screen. This has the effect of making everyone feel they work for the same organisation rather than dozens of independent groups. The intranet helps break down barriers and destroy cliques.

Interactivity

The fourth benefit of an intranet is its interactive capabilities. Workers can communicate with each other in a far more constructive way than with e-mail and problems and projects can be shared and solved using a far greater range of expertise. The level of interactivity will depend on the company policy on the intranet. Some organisations like to have very interactive systems with a constant flow of information back and forth between employees, sharing ideas, comments and innovations; while others prefer a more static version where the users can only access the information without the ability to respond directly. The degree to which an intranet is interactive will probably lie with the managing directors and chief executives, but the facility is there if needed.

The use of 'Bulletin Boards' is an ideal way for employees to share information and ideas. This is where one page of the intranet is used for the users to post their comments and everyone else can view them. However, the intranet editor should always be on the look out for material that may be deemed offensive, actionable or an infringement of copyright. Abuse of electronic networks is becoming increasingly common in the workplace and has led to a number of court cases around the world.

1.8 Assessing the potential market

Most people who have seen or used an intranet would not dispute their potential for being a potent and revolutionary business tool. But how great will their influence be in the future? Any kind of prediction about the development of computers and their role in society is a dangerous business: who would have thought that when a single computer occupied an entire room that in less than 50 years they would become a common addition to both the workplace and the home. The speed of IT development is so fast that it can be precarious making predictions for the future.

An important factor in the future success of intranets is the development of the Internet. In 1996 Bill Gates of Microsoft suggested that the Internet was a fad that would not catch on with the general public. He has since had to radically revise these sentiments in light of the fact that the Internet is making inroads into all sections of society as more and more people look to travel along the information superhighway. However, it is still entirely possible that general interest in the Internet will reach a plateau and then tail off. One of the likely problems is that with too much information on the Internet, people will get fed up with surfing through pages and sites that mean nothing to them. In years to come we may view the Internet, in its present form, as the dinosaur of the IT world as far as the general user is concerned.

Business opportunities

It is the business uses of the Internet that could lead to the long-term success and expansion of intranets. More and more companies are doing business on the Internet and a variety of organisations from universities to churches now have sites of their own. All these organisations recognise the business opportunities of the Internet: marketing, advertising, sales, invoicing and after sales service. It is for these specific services that the Internet really comes into its own and with this comes an increased role for intranets. Intranets offer the possibility of linking internal and external information and, if required, customer-related information held on an intranet could easily be made available to a wider audience via the Internet.

The long-term success and expansion of an intranet depends in part on the systems that are being developed and implemented at present. If they are well thought-out and effective then they will be seen as a great asset in the workplace and be quickly accepted. However, if they are put together in a haphazard fashion with little or no long-term vision then they may be viewed as clumsy and unnecessary. This of course could be improved at a later date but it is always harder to relaunch an initiative than it is to get it right the first time.

If intranets become an established part of our working lives then their potential to transform the way businesses and organisations operate is huge. We may see a genuine move towards the idea of a paperless office (or at least a paper-reduced office) as notices, manuals, newsletters, telephone directories, personal details and training material are transferred to the intranet. In addition, employees will have, at their fingertips, the information that they need to do their job more effectively. This should lead to genuine empowerment, i.e. the power to work for the greater benefit of themselves and the organisation they work for. If intranets continue to grow in the way it has been predicted, then perhaps in 10 or 20 years' time they will have become as much an integral part of office life as telephones, photocopiers and fax machines are today. Intranets even have the potential to replace all three of these.

1.9 Summary

- Intranets are like individual versions of the Internet that are self-contained within an organisation.
- Intranets use the same technology as the Internet but they have a much more specific purpose.
- Intranets are not ideal for all organisations but if there are 100 or more employees involved then they should be a serious consideration.
- Depending on the size of the organisation, intranets can operate within a single office or link employees on separate continents.
- Intranets can bring a variety of business benefits, ranging from a reduction in paper to a better-informed workforce.
- Although an intranet can be installed in a matter of a few weeks (in theory) it is better to take your time and make sure that the planning and implementation is well thought out.
- Intranets should be seen as a long-term commitment, not a short-term quick fix.
- Be prepared to make a personal commitment to introducing an intranet and accepting both criticism and praise.

1.10 Checklist

1 Find out as much as you can about the intranet concept. Computer magazines are a good source of material as are the information technology supplements that most broadsheet newspapers carry in their midweek editions. The Internet also has a wealth of information on its business-orientated cousin. Simply type in the word 'intranet' into one of the search facilities (a search engine) and wait for the number of applicable sites to appear.

2 Decide whether your organisation is suitable for an intranet. If you are self-employed as a one-man business then it may not be appropriate. However, if you are in an organisation with over 100 employees then it may be worth looking into.

3 Make sure your organisation has the technical capabilities to handle an intranet. Basically this means personal computers, or the equivalent, linked by a network, because if you have this then the rest can be added relatively easily.

4 Look for areas of your organisation that could be improved by an intranet: reducing paper and printing costs, improving staff awareness and keeping information current and up-to-date.

5 If in doubt, seek the advice of organisations that already operate intranets.

2 | PLANNING AN INTRANET

2.1 Forming a project team

If there is one word that best describes an intranet, it is 'egalitarian'. It is a communications system that can be used by everyone in an organisation and they can all enjoy it in the same way. There should be no cliques, inner circles or petty point scoring as far as an intranet is concerned. Because of this it is essential to include as many areas of your organisation as possible, if not all of them, in the planning stages of setting up the system. A project team should be created with representatives from all of the key areas in your organisation. The reasons for this are threefold:

1 If all areas are included then everyone will feel as if they have an active role to play in the development of the system and that it is not something that is just being forced on them.

2 Employees from different areas will have an expert knowledge of their own section or division. As a result they will be able to offer advice about what people in their area will want to see on the intranet.

3 If there are representatives from throughout the organisation then these people could be used as contact points once individual areas start creating their own pages for the intranet.

The first task to perform with the project team is to create a clear hierarchy of responsibility for who does what. This will include deciding who has ultimate control of the content of the intranet and who is responsible for the technical side of the system; the nature and style of input from separate areas; and a clear structure for creating, editing and revising pages on the intranet. Initially it will be the role of the person who is promoting the idea of the intranet (ideally someone from a communications background) to explain the system and what it is, and is not, capable of doing. The project team should then assess this new tool at its disposal and calculate how it can be best used for the overall benefit of the organisation and its employees. This may involve going and canvassing employees to see what they would like on the system, because it would be counterproductive if the project team itself was seen as a secretive clique.

At every step of the way, the project team should report clearly and openly and always be prepared to listen to the views of other people. Openness and inclusiveness from the very beginning are vital to an intranet project getting off to a positive start.

2.2 Writing a proposal

Even with all of the planning in the world, your intranet will come to nothing if you cannot persuade the powers-that-be in your organisation to authorise the installation of such a system. This means that you will need to convince the management on two fronts: one, that an intranet will promote the business needs of the organisation and, two, that it will be cost effective. It is a fact of modern business life that any new initiative has to be justified with hard facts and a persuasive business argument. You will have to do this with your proposal for an intranet.

When putting together a business proposal for an intranet you should consider a two-pronged approach: a written document that will contain all of the relevant information and also a demonstration of an intranet, including half a dozen pages that illustrate the format and capabilities of the system. This way, the people making the executive decisions can see a working example of an intranet in addition to facts and figures in a report. Your written proposal should cover the following areas:

- General information about what an intranet is
- What is required to install and run an intranet
- A list of the benefits it can bring to an organisation
- The type of cost savings that can be made
- Some organisations that already operate intranets

Since in effect you are trying to sell your idea to management, you are allowed to be as persuasive as possible, while not making any outrageous claims that you will not be able to back up. Begin with a very basic description about an intranet. Concentrate on the idea that it is a local Internet and will produce your organisation's very own equivalent of the World Wide Web. Most people in business have heard of the Internet so this is a useful reference point for beginning an overview of an intranet and what it does.

Having set out what an intranet is, you should then detail the technical requirements for the system: servers, browsers and desktop computers of a certain specification. Include costs for all of these items because no matter how impressive your argument is, management will be particularly interested in how much it will all cost. Since the computers will undoubtedly be used for a variety of activities, this is a cost that should not be totally allocated to the creation of an intranet.

Highlighting the savings

On the subject of cost, one of the biggest selling points of an intranet should be the financial savings that the system will bring. These should be broken down into tangible savings and intangible ones. The tangible savings are those on paper, printing and distribution costs and if possible you should try and work out an estimate for this. Take an item such as general notices or the office newsletter and work out how much paper and subsequent costs your organisation would save if these were placed on the intranet. Initially these might seem like fairly small figures (a few hundred or thousand sheets of paper perhaps) but if you begin to include other items such as manuals and training material then the end figure may even surprise you. For a final figure, use at least a three-year timescale. This not only produces a more impressive prospective saving but it also shows that you are not just planning an intranet for the short-term.

The intangible savings include improved staff morale and having a better-informed workforce. Neither of these should be treated lightly. A motivated and happy workforce is becoming increasingly recognised as having a major impact on the success of any organisation. If the staff have a better understanding of what they are doing, this will be a benefit both internally and in terms of improved customer services. For both the tangible and intangible savings your proposal should include specific examples with hard facts to back up your argument.

Even if your proposal meets with a favourable response, the people who make the decisions will want to know about organisations who already have intranets and how they work — it is all very well being innovative but it is also nice to know that you are not the only one trying something new. Compile a list of organisations that already operate intranets (business, educational establishments, public sector departments and charitable organisations) and include this in your report. Names of these organisations can be found on the Internet (try searching under 'intranet users') or in articles about intranets in computer magazines or the IT supplements that most newspapers carry these days.

When you are writing your intranet proposal you should remember that you will be competing against other new ideas and initiatives. Make your report as punchy and persuasive as possible – you are trying to sell something, so give it your best shot.

2.3 Deciding on your message

When planning an intranet the first task is to decide what type of information to put on it. Because of the power of the intranet, the sky is the limit as far as communication is concerned – it can be as simple or as complex as you like.

Before any work on a system is undertaken it is worth stressing that the cornerstone of any intranet is the accuracy of the information it holds. If items are inaccurate or out of date then users will very quickly realise that the system is unreliable and so stop using it. The accuracy of data should be the starting point for any project team.

It is worth remembering though that whatever you put on the intranet can be available to all staff at the same time. This is an example of *Pull* communication where the user can access the information by pulling it from the system. This replaces the more traditional system of *Push* communication where information is pushed out from the top and slowly cascades down through the various levels of seniority. Pull systems of communication allow the users to look at exactly what they want, so the information that they choose is more specific to their actual jobs. Push communications tend to be a bit more hit and miss as they rely on people putting out information that they 'think' employees need to do their jobs more effectively. While Pull systems are more efficient, as a rule they work best in conjunction with aspects of Push systems, such as briefings and one-to-one communications.

In general there are two routes to go down when choosing the type of intranet you want to produce:

1 A read-only intranet that informs employees about the company.

2 An interactive intranet that allows employees to air their views.

Using a read-only system

A read-only intranet is the easiest, and cheapest, to install and run. But even so, some careful thought needs to go into what is going to be put on it. It should be information that gives staff a better idea of what goes on within the organisation and so allows them to do their jobs more effectively. As with every other consideration about an intranet, the type of information put on the system should have a direct relevance to the work of the organisation. Do not put on information just for the sake of it or include a device just to show off your ability to use gimmicks on the intranet.

A read-only system could include information such as:

- **Telephone directories** – enabling employees to find the right number first time and also route external telephone calls accurately.

- **Annual Reports and Accounts** – allowing employees to have a better overall understanding of the company.

- **Product information** – enabling employees to pass on up-to-date information to colleagues and customers. This can be an invaluable business benefit and also very important if there are people out of the office, such as salespeople, who need to check up on the latest product information.

- **Relevant press cuttings** – giving employees a better overall understanding of the industry in which they work.

- **Training opportunities** – allowing employees to see how they can improve their own development and performance. The intranet is also an ideal medium on which to have online training. It allows employees to participate in training courses at their desks, which has the great benefit of eliminating travel and subsistence costs.

In addition, general information can also be added. This could include items such as internal newsletters or magazines; social news; leave arrangements and a noticeboard for small advertisements and personal messages. All of these things could be classed as non-essential, but if they give people a better understanding of the organisation, makes them feel more valued or improves morale, then they have done a useful job.

Do not overload your intranet with every available bit of information you can lay your hands on – every item should serve a purpose, and waffle on the intranet is just the same as waffle anywhere else. The free-spirited approach of the Internet is not appropriate for the intranet. People will be using it as a work tool and as such they want to be able to see what they want, when they want it. They will not have time to read a dissertation about Aunt Bessie's walk along the Great Wall of China, or look at a page that changes colour every 15 seconds. Keep this in mind and make sure that every piece of information that is placed on the intranet serves a legitimate business purpose.

Acting with the interactive

If you decide on an interactive intranet then you have slightly greater scope for innovation. An interactive system can contain all of the same information as a read-only one but in addition:

- It allows the users to create their own pages, share problems, discuss innovations and generally share information.
- It also allows you to ask for feedback on the intranet about specific business projects and survey staff via online questionnaires.
- If your intranet is fully interactive it can also include training via video conferencing.

Levi-Strauss has an interactive intranet that will eventually cover its 37,000 workers in 46 countries around the world and this results in a constant flow of ideas throughout the company. While this can produce a slightly anarchic feel to the intranet (although there are certain guidelines imposed by a global editor), it means that the message throughout the company is one that comes from, and belongs to, the workforce. This means that employees accept the information on the intranet more readily, as they know it is not all generated from a managerial source.

On a more prosaic level, giving employees an interactive role can lead to the generation of more accurate information. If an employee can view and update their own personal details, including items like bank details, marital status, job title and telephone extension, this allows Human Resource divisions to get on with other work. Of course, this puts the onus on individuals to amend their own personal records but it gives them a greater feeling of involvement and 'ownership' of the intranet. Data protection should be borne in mind. Different countries have their own data protection legislation, and you should always be careful not to display unnecessary or sensitive information when you are dealing with personal details.

Weighing up the two systems

Ultimately, the content of an intranet should belong to the people who use it. In its early days the message may be what senior management want their employees to see but as the intranet develops, this should evolve to include the views and ideas of the users. However, there are always advantages and disadvantages to an interactive system:

Advantages:

- It offers more flexibility for both the users and the people who run the intranet. If it is a source of genuine two-way communication then everyone knows that they have a way of expressing their views and making themselves heard.

- It serves as a melting pot for ideas and inspiration. Every organisation needs innovation and an interactive intranet can offer a platform for original ideas and also a sounding board for comments on existing ideas and initiatives.

- It has more potential as a business tool. An organisation that stagnates is one that is doomed to failure. If employees feel they have an interactive role to play in relation to the intranet then there is a good chance that they will convey this enthusiasm into other areas of their job.

Disadvantages:

- In theory it can be harder to control. If people from all parts of the organisation are putting their views and ideas onto the system then the sheer weight of numbers could render the intranet ineffective. This is where global editors (or Webmasters as they are sometimes referred to) are important, to monitor the type of information being included and also the amount.

- If you are not careful it can take on a life of its own. In some instances this can have its advantages but if you get to the stage where sections of your organisation are empire-building on the intranet, then it is time to investigate.

- By definition an interactive intranet takes more effort to manage and maintain. This will come down to a question of staff resources but it is definitely an investment that is worth considering. Undertaking editorial control of an intranet is not something that someone should do when they have a spare 10 minutes during lunchtime: if possible it should be a full-time post.

- There is no guarantee that a message will be read as quickly as the memo pinned in a prominent place on the desk, or noted as quickly as a telephone call.

2.4 Dealing with cost

Counting the savings

As with everything in the business world, cost is an important factor when considering setting up an intranet. When adding up the figures it may seem like a large capital outlay but this should be considered against the potential savings that an intranet can bring. These can be considerable – British Telecom (BT) estimate that theirs has produced a return on investment of a massive 1,500 per cent, which would bring a smile to any managing director's face. (Statistics like this are frequently quoted in relation to the intranet and it should be realised that they do not equate to every single intranet operator.)

Looking at the initial outlay

The initial costs are on computer hardware and software:

- **A server**. This is a piece of software that is installed on a computer at the central point of the intranet. The user sends a request for information to the server via their desktop

computer and the server then returns the relevant data.
The cost of servers vary according to the size and complexity
of the system and the number of users. They can start from
around £1,000 and go up to over £50,000.

- **A browser**. This is a piece of software that allows the user
to view the pages on the intranet once the server has sent it.
It acts as a form of translator between the server and the
user. The best browsers (Netscape Navigator and Internet
Explorer) are free!

- **Personal Computers or Apple Macs**, which allow the user
to run the browser and so view the intranet. A stand-alone
workstation can also be used to view an intranet.

- **Firewalls** (if applicable). A piece of software that can restrict
access to parts of the intranet for certain users. It can also
monitor and restrict information that enters the intranet via
the Internet. As with servers, the cost depends upon the size
and complexity of the system that the firewall is protecting.

- **Authoring software** (if applicable). A piece of software that
can create pages for an intranet. Some of these packages,
although very effective, are very simple to use and an intimate
knowledge of computer programming is not required. Also,
as web authoring becomes more popular with general
computer users the cost of these packages has reduced
dramatically. A good quality package that can produce
excellent results costs as little as £100 and there are several
that can be downloaded from the Internet, free of charge.

Going for home-produced

Once the mechanics of an intranet are in place then the next step is to
decide whether to create a home-produced intranet or call in the ever-
ubiquitous consultants.

Initially it might be tempting to pass the whole project over to consultants
and in some cases this may be a good idea (a very large intranet project
would definitely benefit from expert advice). However, producing your
own intranet is not as daunting as it sounds and it is becoming increasingly
common with businesses and organisations. A simple but effective home-
produced intranet can be created through the following steps:

1 Training a minimum of three members of IT staff (to allow for one being ill and another leaving at the same time) in the technical aspects of the intranet. This includes server installation and maintenance, browser installation and maintenance and the input of intranet files (pages) onto the system.

2 Training a minimum of three members of communications staff in the technical aspects of intranet page authoring so they can produce the pages to be given to the IT section when finished. (It is important that editorial control remains with the communication section and the technical aspects of the system are dealt with by IT.)

Once this training has been completed and the relevant equipment bought it is relatively easy and cheap to create and publish a home-produced intranet. With a little practice the mysteries of the intranet are very quickly unravelled.

Consorting with consultants

If consultants are used then the cost will obviously be higher. However, there are advantages to this:

- Better for handling larger projects.
- Expertise can be used solely for a specific part of the project.
- Likely to complete the project more quickly than an internal team that has other priorities to deal with.

The benefits from an intranet have to be offset against the cost of employing consultants and the best idea could be to approach three or four companies and ask them to give you an estimate for designing and producing an intranet to your own requirements. (The use of consultants is discussed in greater detail in Chapter 5.)

Overall, intranets produced by consultants can cost anything from a few thousand pounds to hundreds of thousands to install and produce. But the chance of a return on investment of up to 1,500 per cent should be enough to make anyone in two minds take the plunge.

2.5 Defining your audience

Channelling information

At first sight the audience for an intranet may seem obvious: all employees in an organisation should be given equal access. In many cases this will be what is required, particularly as the intranet is a system suited to giving everyone the same information at the same time. However, there may be instances where you want to identify a specific audience. This could mean:

- Restricting certain information within the organisation.
- Giving limited access to external customers or organisations.

Limiting access

Achieving limited or restricted access can be done by setting up firewalls within the intranet. These are pieces of software that protect certain areas of information. Only users with the relevant access protocol can then access the information behind the firewall. (See Chapter 8 for more on firewalls.)

The issue of restricting information within an organisation is a sensitive one. It could include confidential financial figures or restricted personnel information that only senior managers should see. However, it can be argued that if this information is restricted to a small number of users then it should perhaps be passed on through a different medium, such as personal e-mails and not the intranet. The problem with restricting parts of the intranet is that it makes people suspicious of what is in the restricted area, thus calling into doubt the integrity of what is essentially an 'open' communications tool.

Opening up the intranet

Allowing access to the intranet for external customers is something that can be a very positive move. Through the use of an Internet link, designated customers, business partners, shareholders or suppliers can gain access to specified areas of the intranet. This could include financial or credit information, allowing customers to view their accounts and deal with relevant payments and invoices more promptly and efficiently. Systems such as this are known as extranets.

The thing to remember with an intranet is that, through the use of firewalls, you can make your audience as large or as small as you like.

Monitoring usage

There is a way to check the level of intranet usage without having to stand over each user to see how frequently they are using the system and for what purpose. All intranet server software has a facility that details the number of 'hits' made on each page. One hit is registered each time a user accesses that page. By using this, the intranet editor can analyse which pages are the most successful and which ones need to be revamped. IT departments will be able to install the necessary software to perform this type of monitoring.

2.6 Achieving short-term objectives

Defining your objectives

When planning an intranet it is important to have some specific and attainable short-term objectives in mind. If not, the project may flounder and be overtaken by the everyday priorities that occur in any organisation. It is a good idea to produce a list of short-term objective for the introduction of your intranet system. This could include items such as:

- Training requirements for IT and communications staff
- Production of the intranet pages
- Programme for a pilot study
- Implementation programme for the roll-out to staff

It is sensible to produce a timetable for achieving your short-term objectives and to give each of them a specific deadline. Request regular updates on how work is progressing. If this is not done, staff may look on the project as optional and not approach it with the seriousness it deserves. A timetable should be realistic and accept that an intranet will not be planned and installed in a few weeks. Figure 2.1 shows the stages of planning an intranet.

Your timetable of short-term objectives could look something like this, depending on the size and location of your organisation: (starting from January).

1 By end of March – train members of IT staff in the technical requirements of the intranet. Train members of the communication section in the production of intranet pages. Appoint a liaison officer to work with IT and

communications sections to make sure they are not working to their own agendas, as sometimes happens!

2   By end of May – task communications staff to produce intranet pages that can be used as part of a pilot study.

3   By end of August – task IT staff to install intranet browsers on all relevant computers throughout the organisation. (This is usually no more than a 30-minute job per unit.)

4   By end of October – run a pilot study with a selection of users covering a range of grades and areas.

5   By end of December – analyse the pilot study and, if successful, implement the full intranet.

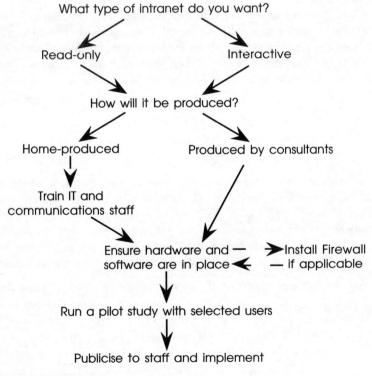

Figure 2.1 Planning an intranet

Once each short-term objective has been achieved, announce it to staff. This not only gets them used to the idea of the intranet but also demonstrates that it is following a structured programme that can be relied upon.

One of the beauties of an intranet is that once your short-term objectives have been achieved your system will be up and running. And, as it does not need months of testing or analysis, it can be cost effective from the word go.

2.7 Setting long-term targets

Planning for the future

Although things change quickly in the world of computing and communications, the planning of an intranet should be seen as a long-term investment.

Long-term targets should be set to measure:

- Financial savings
- Staff performance
- Staff morale
- Customer reaction.

Assessing financial savings

The financial savings consist of both direct and indirect costs. The direct costs relate to savings on paper, printing and distribution costs. In order to assess these over a period of time it is necessary to calculate these costs before the intranet is up and running.

The indirect costs relate to staff time and savings in this can be harder to assess. One way of doing this is monitoring the time taken for directing telephone calls both internally and externally. With an intranet the chances of getting the right person first time are greatly increased, as the directory is accessible to all staff and more likely to be up to date, thus saving both the operator and the caller time.

Improvements in staff performance and morale can either be measured by individual managers who monitor the way people work or it can be done with a staff opinion survey. These are useful for obtaining the views of staff to see whether they feel valued and informed. If you are conducting a survey of this type then include some questions about the intranet – it is useful to hear specific comments about the performance of the system.

Another long-term target is customer satisfaction, leading to increased business. If customers are dealing with an informed and efficient workforce then this will undoubtedly contribute to their overall satisfaction. One of the most common ways to measure the level of customer satisfaction is through a telephone survey. There are companies who specialise in this type of work and it is probably worthwhile seeking their help if this is what you want to do.

2.8 Summary

- The first step in the planning of an intranet should be to appoint a project group, including people from all levels and areas of the organisation. Do not make it too big and make sure that it operates openly and is seen to do so. Once the project team is in place, a proposal for the intranet should be drawn up.

- Keep the idea of accuracy at the top of your list of priorities when implementing an intranet.

- Intranets can be read-only, or interactive, where employees can update information and air their own views and ideas. (Read-only intranets can always be upgraded to become interactive ones at a later date.)

- Decide whether the whole system will be for everyone, or if you want to restrict access to certain parts.

- Consultants can be used and although this will probably result in a slicker product, it will be more expensive.

- It should be clearly defined as to who is responsible for editorial control and who is responsible for the technical requirements of your intranet.

- Have a timetable for planning your intranet. Make sure it is realistic, attainable, but not open-ended. Set a target date for implementation and work back from there.

- When thinking about cost, look at the long-term benefits — as soon as it is up and running it will start saving money.
- Keep the bigger picture in mind. An intranet is not just about saving on paper and printing costs – improving staff performance and customer satisfaction are also central to an intranet's impact.

2.9 Checklist

1 Suggest what you think should be said on the intranet. Concentrate on what is relevant to your organisation. Use the Internet as an example of style for an intranet but keep your own organisation in mind when you are considering the type of content you want.

2 Suggest a style for your intranet. Either go for a read-only system that will be used solely to keep the workforce informed about what is happening in the organisation, or an interactive one which can act as a platform for genuine two-way communication. Leave the final decisions of style and content to your managing director.

3 Consider whether you are going to produce the intranet internally or use consultants. Cost is a major factor in this, as is the enormity of the task that lies ahead. Do not be put off by the latter: with careful planning and a little training, home-grown intranets are definitely feasible.

4 Set yourself some realistic target before you start the project and stick to them. If necessary, set new targets each time you achieve one.

5 Bearing in mind that you do not want your intranet to be a flash-in-the-pan, set some long-term target. Keep this in mind when you are implementing your system. Long-term goals can be very useful for focusing the mind on the present.

3 | WORKING WITH HTML

The system used to create pages for the intranet is called HyperText Markup Language (HTML) and it looks a bit like a computer programming language. The good news is that it is not a full-blown programming language but rather a coding system that is used to format text and graphics. It can be easily learnt by the general computer user and you do not have to be a programming expert, wandering around muttering about C++ and JavaScript, to master it. In basic terms, you create the textual and graphical aspects of your page, then add formatting 'tags' which create the desired result on screen when viewed through a browser. The tags are the code that determines the formatting for a particular piece of text or graphic.

One important feature of HTML is its ability to provide 'links' from one part of the intranet to another. These are shortcuts that allow you to move quickly and easily around the pages on the system, without always having to return to a central point.

3.1 Understanding browsers

Before getting into the basics of HTML it is important to understand about browsers. An intranet browser is the piece of software that deciphers the coded HTML files and allows you to view them in clear, attractive, user-friendly format on screen. Intranet browsers are exactly the same as the one used for the Internet and the two main ones to choose from are Netscape Navigator and Microsoft Internet Explorer. (There are other browsers on the market but realistically these are the two main players.) Netscape pioneered much of the browser technology but since then Microsoft have undertaken a vigorous marketing campaign in order to try and gain control of this lucrative market. Due to the intense competition between the two companies both of the browsers are now provided free of charge.

As far as performance is concerned, both of the browsers provide a good platform for viewing an intranet and, despite the friction that there has been between the two companies, there is not really much to choose between the two as far as the general user is concerned. If you want, you could obtain copies of both of them and see which one you prefer. It may be the case that you will stick with the browser you try first because you will probably feel most comfortable with it. However, there is not much to choose between them, so don't spend too much time agonising over the decision.

A browser is made up of five elements: the main screen, a menu bar, a toolbar, a location address line and a status bar. The main screen is the area between the menu bar, the toolbar and the status bar and will be blank unless it is showing a particular page of an intranet. The location address line appears at the top of the screen and shows the full address of the page that is currently being viewed. The status bar appears at the bottom of the screen and lets the users know what stage of a particular operation the browsers is at e.g. Searching, Done, Could Not Find. Figure 3.1 shows the basic format of a browser (in this case Navigator):

At first sight a browser may look like little more than a jumble of icons and symbols but even the novice user will be able to use it confidently after only a few minutes' practice. There are different versions of the browsers and the appearance and functions of each version is slightly different but essentially they have the same main elements. Navigator and Explorer are similar, but not identical, in appearance and the main differences are in the Menu Bars and Tool Bars. These vary according to the particular versions, but these are the main features:

Netscape Navigator

The Menu Bar

The menu bar appears at the top of the browser and has these options:

File   The commands here allow you to **Open** new HTML files (particularly useful when you are creating your pages and you want to see what they are like as you go along – simply select your file from the relevant directory and see how it appears on the browser); change the **Page Setup; Print** the page; and **Send** and receive e-mail.

Menu Bar

Tool Bar

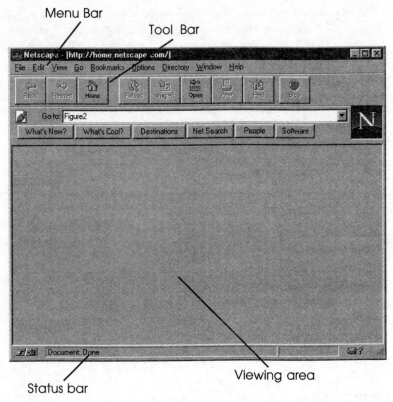

Viewing area

Status bar

Figure 3.1 The basic format of a browser (Netscape Navigator)

Edit   Here you will find the standard functions of **Cut**, **Copy**,
              Paste, and **Select All**, plus **Find**, which lets you search
              for words in the current document.

View   These commands format the appearance of the page.
              Reloading a page displays changes that have been made
              to the source HTML file; viewing the **Source** of the
              HTML document can be very useful if you see something
              you like on a web page and you want to see how it is
              produced in HTML.

Go   This enables you to go straight to certain pages, such as
              the previously viewed one or the Home Page.

Bookmarks   These commands allow you to store links to your most frequently visited pages, and to revisit them easily.

Options   These allow you to change the look of your page by altering items such as the colour of hypertext links.

DirectoryThis menu contains shortcuts to key pages at Netscape's Web site.

Window   These open new windows and run other aspects of the Netscape software package, such as e-mail.

Help   General help information.

The Tool Bar

At first sight the Navigator tool bar seems to be split into two, separated by the location address. Below the address is a line that has buttons named What's New!, What's Cool, Handbook, Net Search, Net Directory and Software. These are tools that are used to connect to pages at Netscape's site on the Internet and so, unless you want to use an Internet link, it is best to hide these buttons. This is done by selecting **Options, Show Directory Buttons** (click to turn this option off), at which point these buttons will disappear from your screen. The rest of the Navigator tool bar buttons are:

Back   Goes to the previous page.

Forward Goes to the next page.

Home   Goes straight to the Home Page.

Reload   Brings up the latest version of the page being viewed. This is essential when you are creating pages: each time you save your HTML file and go to the browser, you must press **Reload** to see the changes you have made.

Images   If you have chosen to turn off the Auto Load Images option (for faster text-only browsing), you can use this to load and display the images in a page. This is one of the few noticeable differences between Navigator and Internet Explorer.

Open   This allows the user to find pages by entering the filename manually. This can be useful if you know the filename and its location within the intranet.

Print   This enables you to print out the current page you are viewing. While this may be considered contrary to the paper-free principle of an intranet it can sometimes prove useful to have a hard copy of a document.

Find   This is the equivalent of the Edit, Find command, and is used for locating words within a document.

Stop   Stops a search for an intranet page. If the search facility cannot find a specified page it will just keep trying, so it has to be told to stop. Also be used to interrupt the downloading of a page.

Microsoft Explorer

The Menu Bar

On the Explorer menu bar the first four drop-down menus are the same, or very similar, to those in Navigator. The **Favorites** option replaces the **Bookmarks** of Navigator.

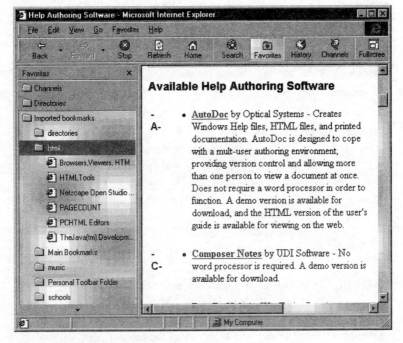

Figure 3.2 Microsoft Internet Explorer

The Tool Bar

This appears under the Menu Bar and is denoted by a row of icons.

Back, **Forward**, **Stop**, **Home** and **Print** are the same as on Navigator.

Refresh	The equivalent of **Reload** on Navigator.
Search	The same as **Find** on Navigator.
Favorites	Lists the pages that you access most frequently.
History	Lists the pages that you have most recently visited.
Mail	Enables e-mail to be sent between users. If you already have an e-mail network in operation then this may not be needed. However, if you do decide to make use of the e-mail facility then you should make this the standard throughout your organisation. It is confusing and unnecessary to have more than one e-mail system.

As browser technology develops quickly it is worth looking at the Netscape and Microsoft Web sites for the latest developments. Find them at:

http://www.netscape.com/

http://www.microsoft.com/

The latest versions of the browsers can be downloaded from these sites and step-by-step guides are provided.

3.2 HTML basics

There are hundreds of sites on the Internet that offer general advice and guidance about HTML. Some to try are:

http://www.quest.internet.co.uk/drh/HTML/index.html

http://www.ncsa.uiuc.edu/General/

http://members.aol.com/Rick1515/index.htm

http://www.pageresource.com/

http://www.microsoft.com/msdownload/#pubtool

Other useful sites can be found by using an Internet search engine, such as Yahoo, and typing in the words *HTML authoring* or *HTML resources*.

HTML can either be created from scratch or it can be produced using a dedicated authoring package. A dedicated package is easier to use and will give impressive results relatively quickly. However, it is a good idea to have a good basic knowledge of how HTML works first. To do this you will need to create some files from the beginning.

To start creating a page in HTML you need a text editor such as Notepad in Windows, or SimpleText on an Apple Mac, or an HTML editor, and a web browser as described above. An HTML editor is much the same as the text editor except that it makes it slightly easier for the user to create the source HTML code.

The Netscape Communicator and Navigator Gold packages include a good HTML editor, Composer, and the Internet Explorer suite contains a similar editor called FrontPage Express. There are other editors on the market and several can be downloaded from the Internet. Two sites to try are:

http://www.webweaver.com/
http://www.faico.net/dida/

The editor allows you to create your formatted HTML file and then you can switch to the browser to see the end result. It is a good idea to check regularly on the browser, just to make sure it is not all going horribly wrong. To move quickly between your editor and the browser you hold down ALT and then press the TAB key once. This way you can jump easily from one application to another.

All HTML commands and formatting are enclosed in tags, which consist of codes written in angle brackets, i.e. '<' and '>'. All HTML elements have an opening tag and most have a closing tag. For instance, to embolden a piece of text you would enclose it with the following tags:

<B>My text</B>

The closing tag always has a forward slash, which indicates that this particular piece of formatting is now at an end.

HTML is relatively logical in its construction: you start with a heading, you add your formatted body copy and then you close your file.

Every HTML file contains certain fixed elements:

- a notification that it is an HTML file,
- a head (which contains the title of the page and may also contain keywords for use by search engines see page 103)
- the body of the document.

So the basic minimum of an HTML file would look like this:

```
<HTML>
<HEAD><TITLE>My first document</TITLE></HEAD>
<BODY>
This is my very first attempt at writing a file in Hyper Text
Markup Language
</BODY>
</HTML>
```

This will appear on the browser as in Figure 3.3.

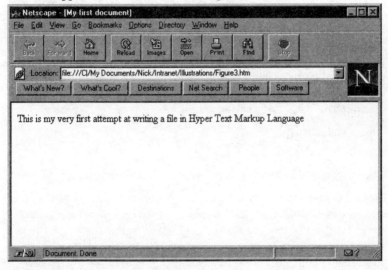

Figure 3.3 Example of a simple HTML file viewed in a browser

The HTML tag identifies what type of file it is. The HEAD area holds information about the page, including the TITLE, which will appear in the top bar of the browser. The text within the BODY tags will appear on the screen of your browser.

The tags are not case sensitive and can be written in either upper or lower case. However, in order to distinguish them, it is a good idea to create them in the opposite case from your document text.

Once your file has been saved (as a plain text file but with an **.htm** extension on a PC or **.html** on a Mac) it can be viewed on the browser.

Make sure your browser is open and move to it using ALT plus TAB. Use the menu command **File**, **Open** and then choose the file you have just created. You will then see your file on the browser. Each time you make a change to your source HTML file you should click on **Save** and then return to the browser and click **Refresh/Reload** on the tool bar. This will show the latest changes to your document.

Paragraphs and formatting

The chances are that you will want to put more than one line of text on your page. HTML has the capacity to separate paragraphs of text, by enclosing them in <P> tags. So you begin each paragraph with <P> and end it with </P>. Do this for each new paragraph that you write.

You can also add specific formatting tags such as bold, italics and underline. To do this, enclose the word or words that you want to format with the relevant opening and closing tags. The three most common formatting tags are:

```
<B>Bold</B>
<I>Italics</I>
<U>Underline</U>
```

Two other useful formatting devices are line breaks and horizontal rules.

Line breaks are indicated by the <BR> tag (this is an exception that does not need a closing tag). This starts the text on a new line – and is particularly useful because HTML does not recognise the RETURN key as a line break. If used after a <P>paragraph</P>, the <BR> tag inserts an extra blank line above the new text.

The horizontal rule tag <HR> (which also does not need a closing tag) inserts a solid line at the point of the body document in which it is inserted.

Using the above formatting devices in an HTML document would result in a source file looking like this:

```
<HTML>
<HEAD><TITLE>My first document</TITLE></HEAD>
<BODY>
<P>This is my very first attempt at writing a file in HyperText
Markup Language</P>
```

<P>HTML is much easier than I first thought and I have already learnt how to add <B>bold</B>, <I>italics</I> and <U>underlining</U>.</P>

I can also insert line breaks

And horizontal rules.

<HR>

</BODY>

</HTML>

This will appear on the browser as in Figure 3.4.

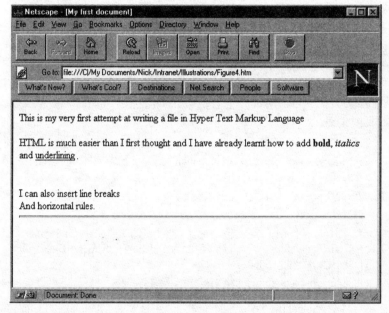

Figure 3.4 Example of basic formatting of an HTML file

Working with text

Having got your initial text on the page you may want to change its appearance. This can be done in two ways: using Heading and other style tags; or defining the font size and type. The Heading tags come in the form <H></H> and there are six levels of hierarchy, from <H1> at around 24 point down to H6 at around 10 point. Text that is enclosed within heading tags will be separated from the next line of text automatically.

The text can be formatted in various ways, using options within the basic
<FONT> tag. If you want to change the font style from that of the system
default you need to specify the new font that you want to use. This is done
with the FACE option, in the form:

```
<FONT FACE="??"> formatted text </FONT>.
```

The fonts that you use must be present on all the computers on your
intranet, if other users are to see it.

If you want to change the size of your text you can do this with the SIZE
option. This can be incorporated within the FONT tag so if you want you
text to appear as Century Gothic in size 4 (14 point) your tag would be:

```
<FONT FACE="CENTURY GOTHIC" SIZE=4>
```

So if headings and text formatting were added to the above example then
the HTML file would look like this:

```
<HTML>
<HEAD><TITLE>My first document</TITLE></HEAD>
<BODY>
<FONT FACE= "Century Gothic">
<H1>This is my very first attempt at writing a file in HyperText
Markup Language</H1>
</FONT>
<FONT FACE= "Arial" SIZE=2>
<P>HTML is much easier than I first thought and I have
already learnt how to add <B>bold</B>, <I>italics</I> and
<U>underlining</U>.</P>
<H3>I can also insert line breaks</H3> <BR>
<H4>And horizontal rules.</H4>
</FONT>
<HR>
</BODY>
</HTML>
```

This will appear on the browser as in Figure 3.5.

Experiment with different heading sizes and font styles to see which ones
best serve your purposes.

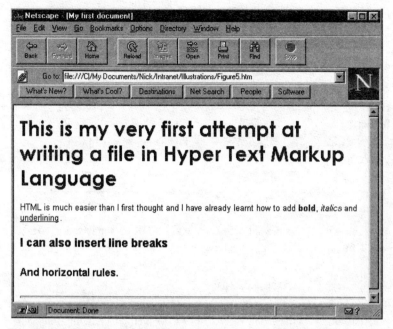

Figure 3.5 Example of more formatting of an HTML file

Background and text colours

Colour is an important part of an intranet site and with HTML you can set the colour of the page background and the colour of the text. Colours are set in HTML using either colour names or hexadecimal numbers. The names are the simplest to use, and are the best choice for standard colours.

Hexadecimal numbers may look almost incomprehensible at first glance, but they in fact follow a simple pattern. Each number contains three pairs of digits which set the amount of red, green and blue in the colour (we're mixing light, not paint!). The digits are the numerals 0–9 and letters A–F, and are the equivalent in ordinary numbers to 0–15. 00 is the lowest, and means no light of this colour; FF is the highest, and gives the colour at full luminance; 80 is approximately the middle value. Any value can be used and will produce its own distinct colour (when viewed on a high colour screen), but just using these three you can create a wide range of colours.

The following table lists the colour names and their hexadecimal codes.

Name	Hex value R G B	Name	Hex value R G B
Black	000000	Gray	808080
Silver	C0C0C0	White	FFFFFF
Red	FF0000	Maroon	800000
Lime	00FF00	Green	008000
Blue	0000FF	Navy	000080
Fuchsia	FF00FF	Cyan	00FFFF
Yellow	FFFF00	Teal	008080
Purple	800080	Olive	808000

(Note the American spelling – Gray.)

Background colours are set using the BGCOLOR option in the <BODY> tag. Thus, for a white page background you would use either of these:

```
<BODY BGCOLOR= "FFFFFF">
<BODY BGCOLOR= White>
```

The code for the colour can be enclosed within inverted commas, and purists place # at the front, e.g. "#FFFFFF". Neither is essential.

Note also the spelling, COLOR – HTML uses American English.

Experiment with different combinations to see the effects you can achieve.

Text colour is denoted in the same way as background colour and can be set in two ways.

- The TEXT option can be used in the <BODY> tag to set the default text colour for the whole page.

- The <FONT> tag can take a COLOR option to set the colour of all subsequent text until it is turned off by </FONT>.

So if you want a white background with black text then your body tag should be either of these:

```
<BODY BGCOLOR="FFFFFF" TEXT="000000">
<BODY BGCOLOR= White TEXT=Black>
```

You could pick out a phrase in a paragraph like this:

```
On Friday we will announce the <FONT COLOR = Red>
Employee of the Month</FONT> - will it be you?
```

It's easier with editors

With most HTML editors you can select the background and text colours directly from a colour palette - far simpler!

3.3 Adding links

A single intranet page can be as sophisticated and interesting as you like but if that is all there is then the users will not return to your site. You need to have a variety of information and give people the means to move effortlessly from place to place. This is where the HyperText of HTML comes into its own. HyperText is a device whereby you can click on a designated piece of text, or graphic, that takes you automatically to an associated page. This is called a link and it is a shortcut device that enables users to navigate their way through the intranet.

Links can be incorporated into either text or graphics: with textual links the words are underlined and in a different colour from the rest of the text, and with graphics the image usually has a coloured border around it to denote that it is a HyperText link. Also, the cursor arrow changes into a hand with a pointing finger whenever it is covering a link. Although the code for a HyperText link looks a bit daunting at first sight it is not as confusing as it first seems.

To create a textual link to another part of the intranet you need to take the text you are using as the link and enclose it in a reference anchor. This takes the form of <A HREF=></A> tags. Next you have to insert the name of the page/file which you want to link to. This is called the Uniform Resource Locator (URL) and is a common feature of HTML. URLs are unique addresses for Internet and intranet pages that allow the users to find that page by typing in the relevant address in the location address bar. The usual format for an URL is: *type://hostcomputer/directory/filename*. So if you want to link to a file called NEWS.HTM then you need to insert this reference within your tags, using the code HREF. With this addition the tag would now look like this:

    <A HREF="NEWS.HTM"></A>

As it is, this will create a link from your source document to the NEWS file, but nothing will appear on the screen to let the user know where to click. To solve this a line of text needs to be inserted. This could simply be one word ("News") or a short sentence explaining what happens when the user clicks on the text ("Click here to go to the news of the day page"). The text is inserted after the filename and before the closing anchor:

```
<A HREF="NEWS.HTM">Click here to go to the news of the
day page</A>.
```

The full HTML file for this would consist of:

```
<HTML>
<HEAD><TITLE>My first link</TITLE></HEAD>
<BODY>
<FONT FACE="CENTURY GOTHIC">
<H1>This is my very first attempt at inserting a link to
another page</H1>
</FONT>
<HR>
<A HREF="NEWS.HTM">Click here to go to the news of the
day page</A>.
<HR>
</BODY>
</HTML>
```

This will now appear as a link at the bottom of the screen as in Figure 3.6. It will be underlined and in a different colour from the rest of the text, normally blue.

Writing filenames and URLs

As a general rule, these should be written in the same combination of upper and lower case letters that appear in the original filename. This doesn't matter if you are working purely within a PC-based intranet as DOS and Windows are not case-sensitive. If the network has a Unix server, or you are linking to a place on the Internet where Unix servers are prevalent, then it is important because Unix is case-sensitive. To a Unix machine, "news.htm", "News.htm" and "NEWS.HTM" are three different files!

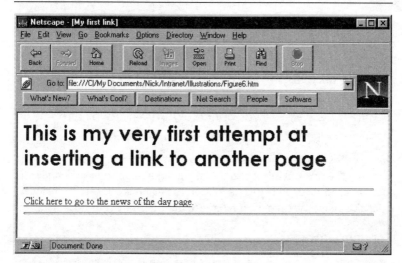

Figure 3.6 Example of an HTML link

3.4 Acquiring images

Graphics and photographs can easily be added to intranet pages and they give an additional dimension to the presentation of the site. However, they should be used thoughtfully and sparingly as they take up more space on the system and so take longer to download. Use them for a specific purpose and make them as small as possible. Background images can also be used to give your pages a textured look rather than just a plain colour. Although this occupies the whole of the background the effect is done by the inclusion of a single image, which is 'tiled' – duplicated across and down – to fill the screen.

Images are stored as individual files that have different extensions (the letters at the end of the filename) according to the format they have been created in. Images can be added to an intranet page in two different formats: Graphical Interchange Format (GIF) and Joint Photographic Experts Group (JPEG or JPG). These are the formats that most web browsers recognise and they both have their advantages and disadvantages. JPEG files can be compressed to take up less disk space and are better for including photographs, while GIF images are better for graphics and icons. Both formats can be obtained by scanning in images, taking them from disk or downloading them from the Internet. There are numerous sites that contain images suitable for the intranet. Try some of the following:

http://www.pixelfoundry.com//bgs.html

http://textures.guinet.com/index.html

http://www.vision-web.net/graphics/

http://www.ip.pt/webground/

http://www.village.vossnet.co.uk/h/henrys/bkex.htm

http://busines.auracom.com/wurld/kitrex3.html

Once you have an image that you want to use on the intranet you should place the file in a suitable directory on your computer. It is a good idea to put it in the same directory as the HTML file that it is going to be included in, as this makes it simpler to reference the file from your documents.

Creating images

Creating your own images is a realistic option if you want to use items such as a company logo or images that are specific to your own organisation. There are two options for doing this: you can either take an existing image and edit it to meet your needs, or you can scan an image and save it as an appropriate file. If you want to edit an existing image then you will need an image-editing program such as Paint Shop Pro or Adobe PhotoShop. These allow you to import an image and then edit it. For instance, if you are producing an icon for a telephone directory you may want to have a graphic of a telephone and the words 'My company's phone directory' underneath. To do this you would import the graphic, add the text and then save the file. Then, when you insert it into your HTML file the image and text will appear as an incorporated icon.

If you want to include a specific photograph or image on your intranet you will need to scan it into your computer. This is done with a scanner, which copies the image and converts it into a suitable format. The scanner will enable you to save the file in different formats and in this instance .JPEG is the best option as it takes up the least disk space. The two main types of scanners are flatbed ones, which look a bit like photocopiers and can scan images larger than A4, or sheet feed scanners which look more like fax machines, as the paper is fed through them. Sheet feed scanners can only use a maximum of A4 sized paper. The price of scanners has fallen dramatically in recent years and a reasonable quality one, with editing software included, will cost as little as £100.

Once you have your scanned image you can then edit it, if you wish, with the software provided with your scanner or one of the editing programs such as Adobe PhotoShop or Corel Photo House. This is a quick and efficient way of adding high-impact images to your intranet site.

3.5 Graphics and background images

Almost all intranet and Internet pages have some images on them, whether they are photographs, icons, bullet points or coloured lines. If they are used wisely, i.e. they are small, serve a purpose and appear in the same style throughout your intranet, they can add an impressive visual impact to your system. However, if you go crazy and start scattering them everywhere, their impact will be reduced and they will become a nuisance.

To include the image (which we will call APPLE.GIF) on the intranet you will need to open your source HTML file. Then add an 'image source' tag. This will appear as:

```
<IMG SRC="APPLE.GIF">
```

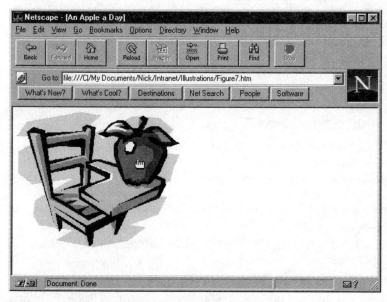

Figure 3.7 Example of inserting an image

The full HTML file for this would consist of:

```
<HTML>
<HEAD><TITLE>An Apple a Day</TITLE></HEAD>
<BODY>
<IMG SRC="APPLE.GIF">
</BODY>
</HTML>
```

If you SAVE this file and then go to your browser and open the HTML file you will see the image appear as in Figure 3.7.

Images can be used as a design element (as above) or they can be used as a link, in the same way as a textual component. As well as including the reference tag for the linking file you also need to include an image source tag for the image that is being used as the link. So to use the APPLE image to link to the file APPLE.HTM the following code would be used:

```
<A HREF="APPLE.HTM"><IMG SRC="APPLE.GIF"></A>
```

If this was inserted in the above example the page would then appear as in Figure 3.8 on the browser (note the box around the image, indicating that it is operating as a link). When the cursor is positioned over the apple graphic the arrow will change to a pointing hand, indicating that it is a link to another page. It is usually possible to check the location of the linked file by looking at the status bar along the bottom of your browser. This will show the name and location of the destination file – in the example it is *APPLE.HTM* in the *Illustrations* subfolder (which is also where this page is stored.)

Some old browsers do not support graphics, i.e. they cannot display them on screen, and some people prefer to turn off the Auto Load Images option for faster browsing. To cater for these users, you can insert an alternative piece of text that will be viewed instead of the graphic. This is done with the ALT code, and to include a provision for non-graphical browsers the HTML would look like this

```
<A HREF="APPLE.HTM"><IMG SRC="APPLE.GIF" ALT="Apple
Image"></A>.
```

If the browser cannot view graphics then the words 'Apple Image' would appear instead and this would be the link. (Note. It is increasingly rare for browsers not to be able to support graphics.)

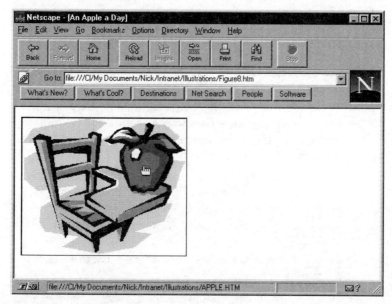

Figure 3.8 Example of an image acting as a link

Filenames and paths

If an image (or linked file) is stored in the same folder as its page, you only need to give the filename. If it is in a different folder, you must also give the path to that folder. For example, if you kept the illustrations in a subfolder called IMAGES and this was within the one containing your page files, then to link to COMPLOGO.GIF you would need:

<IMG SRC = IMAGES/COMPLOGO.GIF>

If the company logo was stored somewhere far off in the system, the path would be even more complicated. Keep life simple! Store images in the same folder, or a subfolder of the one with the pages!

3.6 Summary

- HyperText Mark-up Language (HTML) is the language used to create pages for the intranet. It is easy to learn and you can produce your own HTML page with a minimum of training.

- The intranet is viewed through a software device called a browser. The two main ones to choose from are Netscape Navigator and Microsoft Internet Explorer and they are free. Try each one out to see which one you prefer.

- All formatting for HTML is contained within <tags>, which contain the information that tells the browser how to display the text and graphics.

- A link is a piece of text or a graphic that contains a tag, allowing the user to jump straight to a connected page. It is a shortcut device that makes it easier for the user to navigate around the intranet.

- Graphics can be included in HTML pages but make sure they are necessary and try and keep them as small as possible.

- Graphics can be used for their own sake or act as links to other pages on the intranet.

3.7 Checklist

1 Test your pages on all the different types of monitors in your organisation. You will find that some display the information differently from others.

2 Experiment with different sized headings, text styles and graphics.

3 Decide on an overall style for your pages.

4 Create plenty of 'dummy' pages so that you feel comfortable with HTML.

5 Do not scatter too many links throughout one page – unless it is a 'Contents' page! This will lead to the users having to jump backwards and forwards a lot.

6 Always test pages and links before they go 'live' on the intranet. Do this by using your browser to open the file.

4 | BEYOND BASIC HTML

4.1 Looking at advanced techniques

An intranet created using simple and straightforward HTML files can be effective, functional and successful. However, there may come a time when you want to give your system a little more vitality through the use of devices such as, frames, tables, Common Gateway Interfaces, animations, marquees (text that scrolls across the screen) and multimedia effects. While none of these are essential they do add a touch of glamour to an intranet. If you introduce them over a period of time it is a good way to show that the system is continually developing and improving.

When you are dealing with devices such as multimedia effects and animations it is important to check that the version of the browser that your organisation is using is capable of supporting these features. Browser technology tends to develop in line with the latest applicable software developments. This is fine if you have the most up-to-date version of the browser. But if you are trying to run the latest interactive software on an old version of the browser then you may run into problems. Always test any innovative features on the oldest version of the browser that you have on the intranet before you release your latest piece of handiwork on unsuspecting users.

4.2 Getting into Java

It is virtually impossible to deal with any advanced aspects of intranet page authoring without coming across Java and JavaScript. To some people this is the way ahead for intranet/Internet publishing, while to others it is just a mind-boggling computer language involving applets and other equally confusing terms. So what is Java all about?

Java is a fully blown computer programming language that was first developed by a Sun Microsystems software programmer, James Gosling, in the 1980s. Unlike the hundreds of other software programmes that were written at the time, Java has one major advantage: it is 'platform independent'. This means that it can be run on any operating system whether it is a PC, Apple Mac or a UNIX system. The importance of this in computing terms cannot be underestimated. Before the appearance of Java, programmers had to write different versions of the same program for different operating systems; like writing different versions of the same book for different countries. Java has changed all that, fulfilling the role of the Esperanto of the computing world. Once a Java program has been written it can then be run on any operating system (with the aid of a little technical wizardry), thus removing a major headache for programmers.

For the intranet designer, the creation of Java has enabled them to run a variety of software without first worrying whether it will be compatible with all the computers on their system. Java can be used to write full grown applications, such as word processors. On a smaller scale are Java 'applets'. These small programs can be embedded in an HTML page and run on a browser to perform functions such as sending and receiving questionnaires or running animations. As a programming tool, one of Java's great assets is that it allows for the use of more interactivity on the intranet.

This is equally true of JavaScript, a simpler variation on the Java theme that also enables the designer to change the style and substance of the intranet pages.

Although Java and JavaScript have been promoted heavily throughout the computer industry since 1996, it is perfectly possible to run a stylish and effective intranet without ever worrying about them. However, many major companies around the world, such as IBM and Reuters, do use Java applications on their systems and it certainly adds a state-of-the-art touch to any intranet. If you do decide to go down this route then consult with a software expert. Java programming is complicated and it is not something that an amateur can pick up in a couple of hours over lunch. Talk to the experts and see what they can do for you.

For more information on Java, look up the following Internet sites:

http://java.sun.com/docs/index.html

http://www.developer.com/directories/pages/dir.java.html/

> **Want to learn Java?**
>
> If you want to learn Java, or simply know more about its capabilities, you might like to try *Teach Yourself Java* by Chris Wright.

4.3 Activating ActiveX

Never one to stand still and watch other people come up with potentially revolutionary software, Microsoft have not been slow to develop their own interactive programming language, called ActiveX. It is similar to Java, in that it is a language that can add a greater number of features to an intranet. Since it is a Microsoft product ActiveX currently only runs on Windows operating systems (although this could well change in the future). It works in a similar way to Java in that it adds small programs into an HTML page that translate into interactive features for the users. These features include the creation of pop-up menus and checklists; the inclusion of sound clips; the ability to customise the way individual pages look; and the inclusion of video images.

At present ActiveX is aimed very much at the Microsoft user and more information about it can be found at the following Internet site:

http://www.microsoft.com/com/activex.htm

4.4 Understanding frames

Frames are a device that can be incorporated into HTML files to split the finished page into two or more sections. Each section, or frame, is independent of the others and so one can be edited without changing anything else on the page. Each frame can take up a different percentage of the screen and you can specify exactly how big you want each frame to be. The most common use of frames is to have a lengthy list of contents at the side of a larger piece of text. This way the user can scroll down the contents while still viewing the original text. As with any HTML device that initially seems eye-catching and innovative, their use should be limited. Users can get confused and irritated if there are too many frames performing separate functions on a page.

Creating frames in HTML is a bit daunting at first but it is really relatively straightforward. To create a basic frame, that splits the screen into two sections, you need to create three HTML files. One is the file that creates the frame and the other two are the files that contain the data that will appear in the frames. The frame file does not contain any actual data that is viewed on the screen. It merely acts as a device to split the screen and then allocate which files will appear in each of the individual frames.

A basic frame can be created with the following code and files:

Frame file

```
<HTML>
<HEAD>
<TITLE>Example of a frame</TITLE>
</HEAD>
<FRAMESET COLS= "30%, 70%"> (This spits the screen
vertically. You could use ROWS = to split it horizontally.)
<FRAME SRC= "test1.htm">
<FRAME SRC= "test2.htm">
</FRAMESET>
</HTML>
```

Here the <FRAMESET> tag takes the place of the <BODY> tag in a normal HTML files.

The two files **test1.htm** and **test2.htm** can be created as very simple files as follows:

Test1

```
<HTML>
<HEAD>
<TITLE>Example of a frame</TITLE>
</HEAD>
<BODY>
<H1>This is the smaller of the frames — 30% of the whole
screen</H1>
</BODY>
</HTML>
```

Test2

```
<HTML>
<HEAD>
<TITLE>Another example of a frame</TITLE>
</HEAD>
<BODY>
<H1>This is the larger of the frames — 70% of the whole
screen</H1>
</BODY>
</HTML>
```

When the frame file is viewed in a browser it will appear as in Figure 4.1.

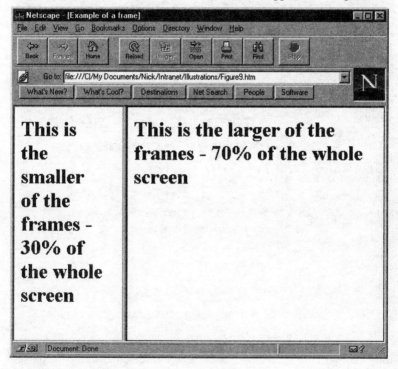

Figure 4.1 Example of a simple HTML frame

Technically you can have as many frames as you like on a page but it is sensible to keep them down to three at a maximum, otherwise things start to get a bit cluttered and complicated. Frames are very useful for contents pages where the main item can appear in the larger frame and the contents can be listed in the smaller one.

Frames are an excellent way to break up pages that have a lot of links in them and they are also useful for varying the visual look of your intranet. If the above frame included more detailed HTML files then the result would look something like Figure 4.2.

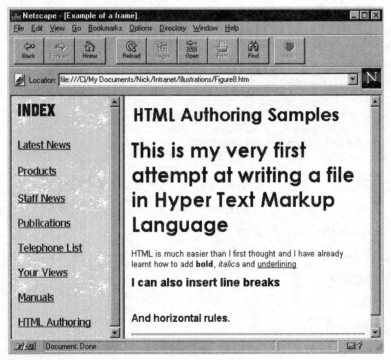

Figure 4.2 Example of a frame displaying two data files

Once the basics of frames has been mastered there are a number of more intricate and complicated variations that can be tried. Information on frames can be found on most HTML resource pages on the Internet; one to try is:

http://www.davesite.com/webstation/html/chap14.shtml

4.5 Using tables

Although tables are optional as far as web page authoring is concerned, they are still an important feature in the web designer's toolbox. Tables allow for data to be presented in rows, columns and cells, giving a much more defined structure to the design of a page. The most obvious application for this is in the production of numerical or technical data, such as in a spreadsheet. However, this is only the tip of the iceberg, as tables on the intranet can be used to align and position large blocks of text and also graphics. This is particularly useful if you want to align a number of graphics, say six, on the same line across a page. Instead of fiddling around with trying to align them all manually you can place them in a table that has six columns. This way you can be certain that the graphics will remain in these positions and they will be properly aligned.

It is perfectly possible to insert hypertext links within tables and the process is exactly the same as putting them into plain text.

As with most HTML, creating tables with a page-authoring package is easier than doing it with manual HTML code. However, even if you are using an authoring package it is useful to know about the elements of an intranet table. (If you are doing it manually, it is absolutely essential.) A basic table incorporates the following HTML tags:

```
<TABLE></TABLE>
```

Marks the start and end of the table defintion.

```
<TR></TR>
```

Enclose each individual row of the table.

```
<TD></TD>
```

Enclose the data (text or image) for each cell in a row. The option WIDTH= can be inserted to specify the width of the cell as a percentage of the row.

Other options to these allow you to set the width and the border style of the table, set the colours within cells, and make cells span more than one row or column – and more – but there is no room to cover these here.

The following HTML code uses these tags to produce a simple table:

```
<HTML>
<HEAD><TITLE>Example of table</TITLE></HEAD>
```

```
<BODY>
<TABLE BORDER CELLSPACING=1 CELLPADDING=7
WIDTH=560>
<!--This specifies the overall width of the table and also the
amount of space around the text in the individual cells.-->
    <TR>
            <TD WIDTH="33%" >This is a basic table</TD>
            <TD WIDTH="33%">which shows how to </TD>
            <TD WIDTH="33%">put text or graphics into</TD>
    </TR>
    <TR>
            <TD>cells and so that they can</TD>
            <TD>be easily aligned and </TD>
            <TD>formatted.</TD>
    </TR>
</TABLE>
</BODY>
</HTML>
```

This would appear on an intranet browser as in Figure 4.3.

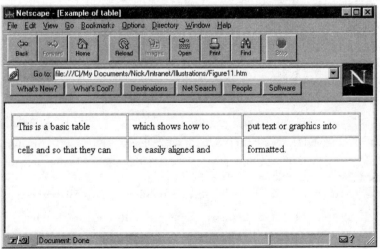

Figure 4.3 Example of a simple HTML table

The code has been indented here to make it easier to see the structure, in particular, the way that the <TD> </TD> tags fit inside the <TR> </TR> tags for each row.

The text written between <!-- and --> is a *comment*. It does not appear on the screen when the page is viewed in a browser.

Table formatting can get very sophisticated. Table and cell lines can be hidden or enlarged; cell sizes can be edited so that they are all equal or separate specific sizes; text can be aligned within cells; and graphics can be added to tables with the text then wrapping around them.

Tables are one of the harder elements of HTML with which to become familiar and confident. When you first start creating tables, take your time to practise and experiment before you start publishing the finished product on the intranet. Although it may seem fairly intricate to begin with, it will become more and more logical and straightforward when you start authoring a variety of different tables. (Creating tables with a web-authoring package is a lot easier since all you have to do is draw the table and then input the relevant data. Even so, it is useful to know what is going on behind the scenes in order to use the software to its full potential.)

Most general HTML sites on the Internet have information about tables and two specific sites to try are:

http://home.tampabay.rr.com/webhelp/tables/
http://members.aol.com/harvillo/tabtut.html

4.6 Common Gateway Interface (CGI)

A Common Gateway Interface (CGI) is a classic piece of computer jargon, the type much cherished by computer buffs and programmers. It means nothing to the man or woman in the street, or even the average computer user, and that is just the way that most of the software programmers would like to keep it. However, a CGI script (a form of program) is a relatively simple and straightforward device that allows intranet users to use the system in an interactive way rather than merely a passive one.

For a user of an intranet a CGI script is a device that allows them to access information within the organisation that is held on computer but is thought not suitable to be permanently on the intranet. It may be archival information that is not relevant to intranet users on a daily basis, or it may be specific and complex data that is only useful to a small number of people. Most organisations have large amounts of information of this kind (usually held in a data warehouse) and a CGI script gives the intranet user the opportunity to view this on their browser. CGI scripts can also be used to enable users to complete and return online forms and questionnaires.

Setting up a CGI script on an intranet is something that is best left to the aforementioned computer buffs. There are considerable technical implications involved in transferring archival information created in a variety of formats into a consistent HTML style. However, as far as the user is concerned the technical aspects can be left to the IT experts while they enjoy the fruits of their labour.

When an intranet user is looking for information from outside the system the CGI script acts as the courier and translator for the data. The initial request is made on a tailor-made form on the intranet browser. This is then sent to the central server where it is picked up by the script. This then locates the necessary piece of information from the data warehouse, translates it into a suitable HTML format and delivers it back onto the intranet browser ready for the user to view.

Figure 4.4 shows the method of operation of a typical data-gathering CGI script. From this point of view it is a simple system. However, it is useful if the users are made aware of a few points before they use a CGI script.

- They should be told the type of information to which the CGI has access. This means they will not waste time looking for data that is not there or have unrealistically high expectations of what a CGI has to offer.

- If the information retrieved by the CGI is updated then the users will need to know how regularly this happens e.g. daily, weekly, monthly etc. Otherwise they may end up requesting information that they have already seen.

- Make sure that the users know how long a CGI takes to operate and return information. This may vary according to the computer networks that are in place and the nature of the request. Test out a number of different scenarios before the CGI is made available to the users.

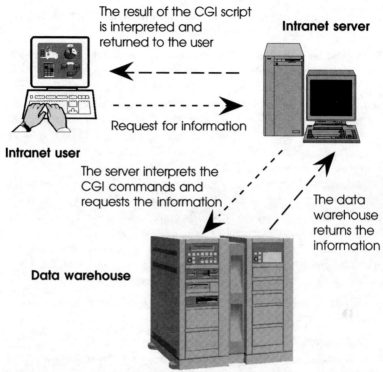

The result of the CGI script is interpreted and returned to the user

Intranet server

Request for information

Intranet user

The server interprets the CGI commands and requests the information

The data warehouse returns the information

Data warehouse

Figure 4.4 Example of how a CGI script works

4.7 Becoming animated

Animations are by no means essential on an intranet and some people view them as irritating distractions. However, sometimes it is good to have a bit of gratuitous fun and animations are one way to bring a lighter touch to the grind of the working day. Surprisingly, animations do not need the combined brainpower of an IT section to create them: with the right tools even a novice web designer could be merrily animating in minutes.

Before trying your hand at becoming the next Walt Disney it is worth considering the role that animations are going to have on the intranet:

- Just for fun? If so, use them thoughtfully and sparingly.

- To catch the user's attention?
- As a recurring theme throughout the intranet? Items such as animated logos could be considered.

The easiest way to create an animated image is to take standard GIF images and then manipulate them with a GIF animation program. These work in a similar way to a cartoonist who draws numerous sets of pictures, each one slightly different from the last, and then creates an animation by filming them frame by frame, one after the other. The animation program will take the GIF images that you have created or selected (you need to have at least two for the animation to work but the more the merrier) and turn them into an animation right before your very eyes. You will be able to edit different aspects of the animation such as speed, colour, background and size. As far as size is concerned, keep in mind how long it takes for each animation to download. It will be longer than a static graphic and the more complicated the animation then the longer it will take to download. There is no point in having a must-see animation if the users log-off before it has had time to download. Having said that, GIFs are ideal for animations because they are small and compact to start with.

Animated GIFS can be downloaded from the Internet; some sites to try are:

http://www.gifanimations.com/animated.shtml

http://www.tiac.net/users/gstudio/an1.html

http://www.wanders2.co/rose/animate3.html

GIF animation programs can be found at the following Internet sites:

GIF Construction Set for Windows

http://www.mindworkshop.com/alchemy/
gcsdemo1.html

Download time

Downloading time is a major consideration when designing pages for the Internet, as file transfer times are rarely better than 5Kb per second and can drop as low as 1Kb per second. The problem should not be as acute on an intranet, though data will move slower on a WAN than on a LAN. Talk to your IT section and find out how fast you can expect to transfer data at normal and busy times.

GIF Animator by Microsoft

http://www.microsoft.com/imagecomposer

4.8 Introducing forms

Online forms are one of the most effective devices for gaining feedback from users and finding out their thoughts about the intranet. The users fill in the form on screen, then press a button and the data is transmitted back to a central point. The intranet editor can then analyse this information. There are three main elements that make up an online form:

- Radio buttons. These give the users the choice of several options and they can select one of them.

- Check boxes. This is where a list of options is provided and the users can select as many of them as they want.

- Text boxes. These are areas for the users to insert their own comments. They can be made as large or as small as required.

Figure 4.5 shows an example of a form where the first question consists of radio buttons, the second, check boxes and the third a text box. Forms can be intricate to create and it is best to consult with your IT department before you try something like this. Alternatively, if you want to find out more about forms then try *Teach Yourself HTML*, in this series.

4.9 Creating marquees

Marquees (small sections of text that scroll across the screen), or banners, are relatively simple devices that can add a significant impact to an intranet. Essentially they both perform the same task, i.e. alert the users to a new or important piece of information that has recently been added to the intranet.

Banners can be created with Java, JavaScript or animated GIFs. Marquees are easier to construct, but can only be viewed through Internet Explorer – they are a Microsoft-specific extension to HTML.

If you want to tell staff that they have just been awarded a special pay bonus then the following piece of text could be placed on the intranet Home Page as a marquee: 'Massive bonus in this month's pay packet!' Using the following piece of HTML code will result in this message catching the user's attention by scrolling across the screen in front of them:

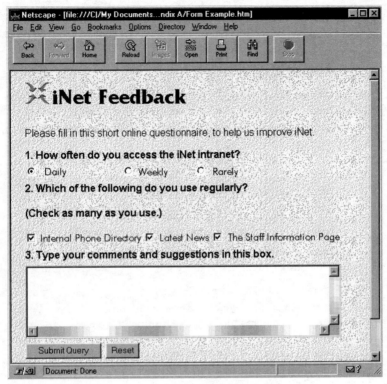

Figure 4.5 Example of a simple form for feedback

<MARQUEE ALIGN= "BOTTOM" SCROLLAMOUNT=2
BEHAVIOUR = "SCROLL"> Massive bonus in this month's pay
packet! </MARQEE>.

Separate elements of the marquee, such as size, colour and speed can
easily be amended to make the message as eye-catching as possible. Some
software programs create marquees and banners automatically. One of
them is the *GIF Construction Set for Windows* (see above).

When using marquees or banners it is important to check that your browsers
can support them. The most recent versions certainly will but if you are using
older versions then they may not be able to recognise the scrolling function.

If your browser does not support marquees you may want to use an
alternative method to catch the users' attention. This could be an animated

GIF saying 'EXCLUSIVE' or 'HOT NEWS', or a static image that is large enough and prominent enough to be eye-catching.

4.10 Web authoring packages

Once you have learnt the basics of creating files in HTML you can, if you choose, forget all about it and head straight for a web authoring package. This is a software program that creates intranet pages on a What You See Is What you Get (WYSIWYG) principle. This means that you create your page as you would with a word processing or desktop publishing application, and what you produce on the screen is what you will see on your intranet page. The HTML code is still all there but it has been generated automatically by the authoring package and you can ignore it completely if you want to. However, despite the simplicity of this it is still a good idea to have a working knowledge of HTML. This will not only make you feel more confident when you are creating your pages but it will allow you to view the source HTML files and alter them if necessary. Also, if your authoring package crashes then you will be stuck if you cannot create HTML code from scratch.

Web authoring packages are undoubtedly a great benefit to anyone who is creating an intranet and for this reason there are a reasonable number to choose from on the market. Most of them also perform site management tasks and this is dealt with in more depth in Chapter 8. Some of the leading packages are:

Microsoft FrontPage

This is relatively easy to use and has a variety of wizards and templates that allow you to design effective intranet pages quickly and painlessly. One useful feature is that it tells you if any of your HTML elements, such as your links, are incorrect and offers advice on how to remedy the situation. As with most Microsoft products, FrontPage has numerous add-ons, such as sound and video applications. It currently costs approximately £125 but a trial version can be downloaded from the Internet at

http://www.microsoft.com/frontpage/default.htm

FrontPage Express is supplied free with Internet Explorer 4.0 and with Windows 98. It has all the page editing functions of the full package, but lacks its web management features.

Versions of Microsoft Word (version 97 or later) also incorporate web authoring functions and while they are not as sophisticated as the dedicated packages they are still very effective and a definite option.

Adobe PageMill

This is produced by the company that is the one of the market leaders in desktop publishing software (they produce the best-selling PageMaker and PhotoShop). It is therefore no surprise that this is one of the best authoring packages in terms of graphics. It also handles text, tables and frames very well and is an excellent overall package, particularly for people who come from a desktop publishing background. It costs approximately £75 at present and more information can be obtained on the Internet at

http://www.adobe.com/prodindex/pagemill/main.html

NetObjects Fusion

This is a more powerful and more expensive package than PageMill but to compensate it does double up as an effective intranet management tool. It can create pages using style sheets and templates and also links the overall style and layout of your intranet. Therefore, if you want to produce the same background on all your intranet pages you only have to do it once with Fusion rather than the unrealistic option of going into each individual file and changing the background. NetObjects Fusion now costs approximately £200 but a trial version can be downloaded from

http://www.netobjects.com/

This is just a small selection of the web authoring packages on the market. If you want to find out the best one for your needs then try downloading the free trial versions from the Internet or contacting the companies to see if they will give you a sample copy.

Putting your pages together

Creating pages with a web authoring package is similar to producing them with raw HTML code, but easier. You begin with creating the overall 'look' of your pages. This is done with wizards that guide you through the whole process of creating a page for the intranet. It will offer you suggestions as you go along and you will be able to accept or reject these. Next, you can type in your text exactly as you would with a word processing application. Feel free to experiment with the size and style of your type and remember – what you see on the screen is what you will get on your intranet.

Adding hypertext links to your text is also ridiculously easy. All you have to do is highlight the text that you want to act as the link, choose Hyperlink from the toolbar and then nominate the file that you want to link to. It is as easy as that. One point to note: try to keep all of your linked files in one directory so that the browser does not have to search too far to find them. Including graphics is also quick and easy: you can copy and paste them from another open file or you can insert them directly from the directory. You can then size and position them as you would in a word processing or desktop publishing application. In addition to the basics, web-authoring packages are also adept at including frames, feedback forms, tables, sound and video.

If you are in the business of creating intranet pages then you should seriously consider investing in a web authoring packages. But first learn how to write HTML files from scratch, if only so that you can fully appreciate the wonder of an authoring package when you come to use one. The one drawback of an authoring package is that it is not as precise as manually created HTML files and so the end product takes up more disk space on the system.

4.11 Summary

- Java is a computer language that can be used to write programs for any type of operating system. It has acquired widespread acceptance by intranet developers because of its ability to insert interactive elements into intranet pages. Its influence could stretch much further than this in the future. ActiveX is a similar type of language from Microsoft.

- Frames and tables can both be used to split up information into more manageable formats for the users.

- A Common Gateway Interface (CGI) script is a device for finding information that is held on the computer system within an organisation but which is not available on the intranet. Following a request from the user, the script fetches the information and then converts it into a format that can be displayed on the intranet.

- Animations are simple to create and they can add a light-hearted touch to an intranet. They should be used sparingly though: not everyone will share your sense of humour and if they are used too much they may become an irritation.

- Marquees create scrolling text that can highlight certain items of information. They too should be used sparingly, to increase the impact of the message, and can only be used if your intranet is being viewed through Internet Explorer.

- Web authoring packages allow you to create intranet pages without any knowledge of HTML. You create a page in the same way as you would a word-processed document and the authoring package converts it into HTML automatically.

- Even with web authoring packages it is a good idea to have some knowledge of how HTML works. This allows you to have a better understanding of what is going on.

4.12 Checklist

1 Ask your IT department about Java and ActiveX, and what benefits they could bring to your intranet.

2 Practise creating frames and tables to see how information can be arranged on screen. Use frames for contents pages and tables for complicated data or when you want to align images or blocks of text.

3 Find out how much archival computer information is held by your organisation. If you think it would be useful for intranet users to be able to access it, look into the possibility of setting up a Common Gateway Interface.

4 Experiment with animations, marquees and banners. Always seek a second, or even third, opinion before you put them on the system.

5 Test some web authoring packages. You may find this easier than creating HTML files from scratch or you may prefer having a full understanding of how your pages are created.

Teach Yourself HTML

There has only been room in this book to cover enough HTML to give you an idea of how it works and what you can do with it. If you would like to know more about HTML, read *Teach Yourself HTML* by Mac Bride.

---

5 CREATING INTRANET PAGES

5.1 Knowing your audience

Before you start designing your intranet you should assess the level of computer literacy throughout your organisation. You may think that the majority of the staff are familiar with computers but the reality may be a little different. If you work regularly with computers then you may think they are the most straightforward, user-friendly items in your office. But other people may not share your confidence and computer awareness. If you presume that most people will know what a web site looks like and understand how to use it then you may be in for a nasty shock. If you launch your intranet on an unsuspecting public and they are uncertain or unsure about how to use it then it could be the end of your project before it even begins. The secret of a good intranet is to always keep the users at the top of your list of priorities.

An easy way to assess computer awareness is by a simple questionnaire. This should include no more than ten questions, each with a YES/NO answer and a space for comments at the end. Keep the questions on general computer issues but also include a few intranet-related items. Some sample questions could be:

- Do you use a computer at work?
- Do you use word processors, spreadsheets, databases or graphics packages?
- Do you think computers are useful for internal communications?
- Do you feel confident with a computer?
- Have you heard of intranets?
- Have you seen a web site?
- Do you think an intranet would be useful in the office?

- Do you use e-mail?
- Do you know what a web browser is?

Send your questionnaire to a sample of at least 30 people or 30% of the staff (whichever is the smaller), selected from throughout the organisation. Include all levels of staff, because the intranet is not a hierarchical device and it should be available equally to everybody. Once you have the results of your survey, analyse them and arrange for any relevant training. (It is worth bearing in mind that some people may be reluctant to admit to having only limited knowledge of computers.)

- If there is a lack of computer confidence among the workforce then some general computer training should be undertaken.
- Irrespective of this, some basic intranet training should be given to all members of staff so that they are not taken unawares when this new medium appears on their computers. This could take the form of a short demonstration or could be done by a handout detailing what an intranet is, the benefits that can be gained from it and how to use it.

5.2 Page design

One of the most common faults in web designing is over-elaboration. In most cases, the maxim, 'less is more' creates an effective and useable intranet site. There is no point in having a site that is festooned with photographs if it takes several minutes to download or causes the system to crash when it is accessed. When designing the site, keep in mind the golden rules of web design:

- Keep it simple
- Be consistent
- Be concise.

Keeping it simple

Simplicity is the key to an intranet site. With the capability of producing pages with photographs, animations, spinning graphics and blinking text the urge for the web designer to get carried away is considerable. Resist it! An intranet site should be viewed for the long-term and therefore it is vital that the pages do not take a long time to download. This means that when the user accesses them they do not have to wait several minutes while their computer recreates your latest animated masterpiece.

A page that takes a long time to download may be mildly irritating the first time but when the user accesses it for the twentieth time they will be ready to cast their computer into oblivion. More importantly they may give up on the intranet as a means of communications.

If you are going to use photographs or intricate graphics then make sure they serve a practical purpose and alert the user beforehand if the page will take a significant amount of time to download – over 20 seconds for most intranet users. Depending on the format, photographs need not be prohibitively large. Make sure you know the size of a photograph (in bytes, kilobytes or megabytes) before you use it.

How long to download?

To find the download time, take the file size and divide it by the average data transfer time on your network.

Maintaining consistency

Like any other corporate document, consistency is important for the intranet. This means that set elements such as background style and colour, text, use of icons and any corporate logo should be the same, or at least recognisably similar. This is not only good practise as far as corporate image is concerned; it also enables the intranet user to feel at ease with the system, as they become familiar with the style.

It is also important to be consistent in your use of links. For instance, if you want to have a link back to your Home Page on every page, then make sure this is maintained. In addition, keep the link in the same style and position on the page. If one link to the Home Page is as an icon at the top of the page then do not have it as a textual link at the bottom of the next one. If you make the users feel at ease with the intranet then they will be encouraged to use, and keep using, the system.

Being concise

Do not fill up pages just for the sake of it when creating your intranet. This is true for any type of business communication but particularly true of an intranet. Since all of the information is displayed on screen it is sometimes more effective to have shorter pieces on each page. This way the user does not have to scroll a long way down the screen to read the whole document. This makes it harder to read and irritating for the user. If possible, try to avoid large swathes of text that the user has to wade through on screen. If you do have a long textual document that you want to put on the intranet then try splitting it up into manageable sizes and using a *Next* and *Previous* link to move from page to page.

Because intranets allow for a huge variety of information to be put on-line this does not mean that you have to take every paper-based document in your organisation and put it on the intranet in its entirety. A little editorial control and judgment is needed. For instance, manuals and reports are popular items for inclusion on an intranet. This is all well and good, but do you need a weighty document like this on your system? In some cases the answer may be yes but in other circumstances it may be beneficial to edit the document and only include the most relevant sections or items. This may seem like a waste of an intranet's potential but the reality is that hard copies of long documents are easier to read than information on screen. In cases like this, think in terms of producing a version that is specifically designed for the intranet – you may even find that a lot of the original document is unnecessary or irrelevant.

5.3 Creating your Home Page

The Home Page of an intranet is the contents page that shows the user what is available. It can appear in a variety of styles, from the conservative to the quirky, but whatever the style there are always some fixed elements:

- The name of your intranet, e.g. MyWeb
- The name and logo of your organisation
- A brief line about the purpose of your intranet
- A group of icons or words that link to the main subject matter
- Some help information about using the intranet
- The name, telephone number and e-mail address of the intranet editor

A Home Page should be welcoming without being intimidating. It should make a new user feel confident about using the system and enable an experienced user to go straight to the information they are seeking. Avoid photographs or complicated graphics as these can take a long time to download and their novelty will wear off very quickly.

Two choices you will have to make are about background and text. The type of image you want to create should govern this:

- If you want a modern, fresh image then you should go for a bright background and a modern typeface.
- For a more conservative image you will want a more subdued background and a more traditional typeface.

Whatever you choose, make sure that the text and any icons are easy to read on your background colour. There is a wide range of background styles that can be incorporated into an intranet. These are available with graphics software packages or can be downloaded from the Internet.

The most important part of a Home Page is the contents portion, that takes the user into the body of the intranet. This consists of either navigational text or icons that the user can click on to take them to the relevant section in the system. Whether you use text or icons to link to the material in your intranet is a design decision for you to take, but unless you want a strictly functional site then you should consider using some icons.

One of the faults of some Home Pages is that too much initial information is put on them, giving a cluttered and unappealing appearance. It is certainly important to include all of the relevant sections but you do not want the user having to scroll through pages of information just to start their search. Keep the main headings to topics such as *Publications*, *Training, Human Resources* then expand on these on subsequent pages. Ideally, a Home Page should have everything visible on one screen.

An important item on the Home Page is a *Latest News* section. This gives the latest information, whether it is a news item or an indication of a new page or section that has been put on the intranet. This should be eye-catching (perhaps the wording 'What's New' in a starburst) and it is vital that it is date-stamped and updated regularly. If there is one thing guaranteed to illustrate a lack of commitment to an intranet it is 'new' information that is weeks, or months, out of date. Set aside time every week to ensure that the information on your intranet is current and up-to-date. This includes the design of the Home Page itself if you think it could be improved, but be careful not to change the overall image.

Some basic design skills are important when creating a Home Page. A few guidelines to follow are:

- Black, white and red are effective on screen. Yellow is also a good background colour on which to put text.
- Avoid similarly coloured text and background together.
- Avoid large amounts of text in all capitals. Use bold or italics for emphasis.
- Do not use more than two typefaces.
- Keep it simple – 'Less is more'.

Figure 5.1 shows a sample intranet Home Page, with each of the items acting as a hypertext link to a particular area.

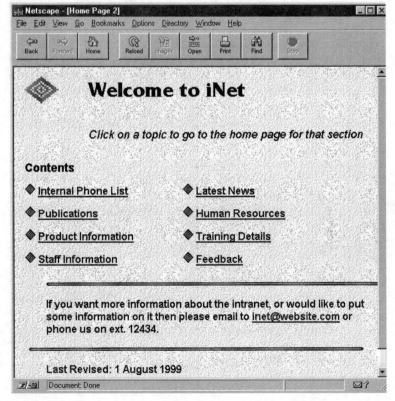

Figure 5.1 Example of a simple intranet Home Page

5.4 Getting into the body

Once a Home Page has been created, it is time to look at what is going to be in the body of your intranet. Ideally the Home Page should have links to the main items on the intranet and these will then have their own home pages. For instance, on the Home Page there may be an icon for *Manuals*. Once this has been clicked on, it will take you to the Manual Home Page which will list all of the manuals that are on the system. You can then click on the one you want and you should see a general index for this manual.

In general, keep your pages in a logical order so the user can go through them step by step to their destination. Keep the most important information easily accessible. For instance, if you have a telephone directory then this should be on the Home Page and not hidden away at the end of a route for *General Information*.

As well as having a logical structure for your intranet (think of it as a tree with branches going off from the main trunk) it is important to allow short cuts to other sections on the system. This can be done by inserting hypertext links in the text so the user can go straight to any related material. This should be done logically and sparingly. Do not clutter up a page with related links or else the user will spend their whole time jumping back and forth from the page they started on.

In addition to thinking about the structure of the pages on your intranet it is also important to pay attention to the style of them. Try and maintain a common design theme throughout and be consistent with features such as the use of your company name and logo, backgrounds, headings and subheadings and typeface size. Draw up a style guide for pages on the intranet and if individual divisions or departments are creating their own pages then make sure they follow a set of guidelines.

Before anything new is put on the intranet it should be checked by the intranet editor to make sure it complies with the house style for content and design. Contributors should be aware of their own responsibility for the content of what they create, particularly regarding actionable comments, and the publication of personal details.

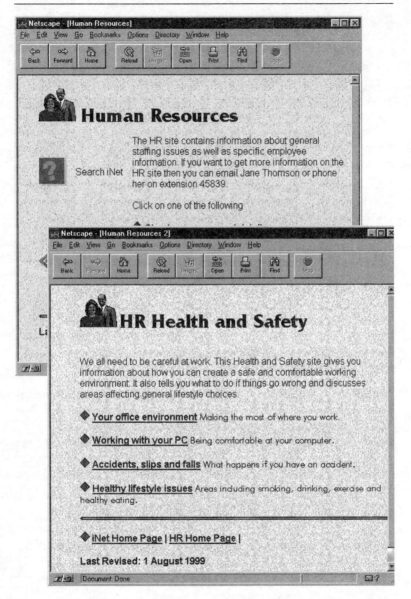

Figure 5.2 The Home page and a follow-up page for one division — note the consistent style.

Templates and style sheets

For consistency of style, create templates containing the common elements and basic formatting – possibly from 'style sheets' (definitions of the fonts, colours, sizes and other formatting options to be used for tags). The template file can be distributed to all contributors, to be used as the basis for their own pages.

5.5 Exploiting links

The effective use of HyperText links in an intranet is vital to its success. Not only do they provide a quick, easy and efficient way for the user to navigate from page to page, they also inject a vibrancy and dynamic element into the system. No longer is it just a static screen of information: it is a compliant information system that is on the side of the users, not against them. Links are written into the HTML program and can appear as text, graphics or buttons. They can be the size of a small bullet point or they can take up most of the screen. Figure 5.3 illustrates how intranet pages can be linked together.

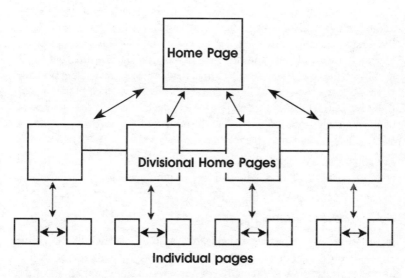

Figure 5.3 Example how intranet pages link together

In order to make the best use of links, some careful thought needs to go into their style and positioning. As discussed earlier, links can either be in textual or graphical form. In general it is best to stick to graphical links for icons linking to main topics, i.e. the items on the Home Page or links to the Home Page of another major section. Graphics have more impact, and – as long as they are well designed – provide an easily recognisable link. If you are linking to an item within the same section, or even the same page, then it is better to keep to textual links. This helps to emphasise that the movement is within the same area.

The positioning of links is also an important consideration when looking to create an intranet site that is easy to navigate around. You want the user to always feel in control and that they can move to another part of the intranet at any time they want to. The worst case scenario is to have the user floundering on a page, unsure of where to go next or how to get out of the page they are on. Of course they can use the HOME or BACK buttons on the toolbar but this is not necessarily an ideal solution. It is the job of the page author to use links as logically and effectively as possible.

Links to the Home Page

The first step in the effective use of links is to make sure that the user can always go straight back to where they came from. Initially this means having a link back to the Home Page. One mistake that is often made with Home Page links is that they are inserted at the end of the file. This seems perfectly logical if the user always finds the right page they want first time, but this is not always the case. It is perfectly normal for a user to select an item from the Home Page and then decide that it does not really satisfy their requirements. If this happens they want to see a link back to the Home Page right in front of them and not have to scroll down to the bottom of the page they are on, or select *Home* or *Back* from the toolbar.

Links back to the Home Page should always appear in the same format and as a design feature it is no bad idea to put then at the top and bottom of every page on your system. If nothing else it offers a comfort to the user.

Links to section Home Pages

In the same way that there should always be a link back to the Home Page, so too should there be a link to the first page of any major section on your intranet. For instance, if you have a site for Training, all of the pages within this category should have a link to the Training Home Page.

So if you are looking up the latest training courses available then you can easily return to the beginning and switch to the another, related, category. Do not be afraid to put more than one link at the top and bottom of your page and include forward links as well as ones to previously visited pages.

Links to other pages

Links within a file to other pages are useful for two purposes: breaking up large items of text and cross-referencing to other relevant material. As a tool for dissecting text into manageable chunks, links are invaluable. Instead of having to scroll down through pages and pages of text, links can be inserted throughout the document to allow the user to skip conveniently to the next part of the article. This is done by inserting *Next* and *Previous* links at appropriate points throughout the text. Of course the page author will have to separate the text in different files but for the user there will be a seamless transition from one page to the next. As a rule, try and avoid having to scroll down more than two 'screens' of text, it is time-consuming and makes it harder to read. If possible, keep a whole page on screen and include a link to the next page at the bottom.

How big is a screenful?

The amount that will fit onto a screen depends upon the size of the screen, the size of the window that the browser is running in, and the size of the text as seen in the browser (users can change the font size). As a general rule, you should set up pages so that they work well when viewed on the computer of an average user — and that may well have a lower specification than yours.

Cross-referencing

As a cross-referencing tool it is possible to insert links into the body of a piece of text. When dealing with where to put links in this instance it is a good exercise to read through a hard copy of the text and underline key words that you think are particularly relevant to the topics. Try and be selective and avoid the temptation to litter every paragraph with numerous links just to make sure that you have covered all the bases. This will result in the user becoming dizzy as they dart back and forth between the original page and the linked material.

Links within pages

If you decide to have pages that require a lot of scrolling you could consider putting links to other parts of the document. This acts as a shortcut, allowing the user to quickly skip to the parts of the article that they want to read. Although it is usually better to split long documents into different files, linking within a page can be a marginally quicker way to navigate through long pages of text since they do not have to go in search of another file.

For example, if you have a source file called manual.htm and you want to have a link from the top of the page to a section called *Technical* then you would insert the following code at the beginning of the file:

```
<A HREF=manual.htm#Technical>Technical</A>
```

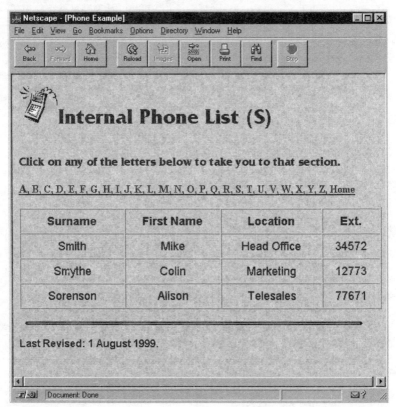

Figure 5.4 Long files should be split into manageable sections

Then, at the point you want to jump to, the following code is inserted around the relevant word or phrase:

```
<A NAME=Technical>Technical</A>
```

So when the user clicks on the highlighted word *Technical* at the top of the document they will automatically be linked to the relevant section.

5.6 Working with graphics

Just as with everything else on the intranet, graphics and photographs have to serve a specific purpose and have business benefits in mind. So if a graphic is small, clear and makes it easier for the user to find their way around the intranet then it has served its purpose. However, if it is clumsy, slow and creates confusion then it is acting against the goals and aims of the system. Make sure that graphics are easily identifiable with the subject to which they are connected i.e. a telephone graphic for a telephone directory. And remember, size does matter as far as the intranet is concerned: the bigger the graphic then the slower it will be to download, wasting valuable time and thus creating an irritated employee.

Photographs on the intranet are an even more sensitive issue than graphics, simply because they tend to take up more disk space. Use them to denote events of special interest to your organisation i.e. if someone has received a special award or excelled in a sporting event. As a rule, keep them to a minimum and use them as a special treat for you and your users.

5.7 Using consultants for page authoring

Whenever you are dealing with HTML and web authoring the question of consultants will raise its head sooner or later. Most people have fairly fixed opinions about consultants, they either love them or they hate them. With the creation of an intranet there is no clear-cut case one way or another, but the increasing versatility of HTML editors and web authoring packages mean that there is no absolute necessity for any organisation to use consultants. Despite this there is an ever-increasing number of IT consultants who are offering their services for the creation of intranets.

The thing that consultants do best is create slick, professional pages for your intranet. The end product will almost certainly be impressive, and if it is not, you can always ask for a second version. Where consultants perhaps fall down a little is with their propensity to dazzle the client with professional jargon and techno-speak. Once they have told you about the latest state-of-the-art software and the amazing things it can do you may feel that this is vital to the success of your intranet. If you then sign up you may find yourself with enough technical wizardry to launch a space shuttle, and a price tag to match.

Taking control

The first thing to do when interviewing prospective consultants for your project is to let them know who is boss. You are the client, so the system you are looking for should be tailored to your specifications. After all, you are the one who knows all about your own organisation, not the consultants. Before you talk to anyone, draw up a list of what you want from your intranet and what you regard to be superfluous. For instance, you might want a read-only system that has no interactive elements or you may want one that will allow for comments and feedback. Listen to what the consultants have to say, but be firm and stick to what you think is best for your system and your organisation.

When discussing technical requirements for your intranet it will be to your advantage to have a sound knowledge of how the system works. A good basic understanding of HTML, servers and browsers will demonstrate to the consultants that you know what you are talking about and that you are not prepared to have the wool pulled over your eyes. If you have learnt the system from scratch then you will be able to discuss your project on a level playing field. It is also a good idea to have someone present from your IT department so that they can deal with technical aspects of the overall system.

On the surface, the pros and cons of using IT consultants for producing an intranet seem to boil down to cost against quality. However, consultants thrive on maintaining the sense of mystery about their own speciality. If you can break this down by researching as much as you can about intranets you may discover that they are not as complicated to produce as some people might have you believe. You already have a head start with your knowledge of your organisation and what you want from an intranet. If you can harness this with some basic IT knowledge and a clear concept of what you want then you are well on the way to producing an effective system on your own.

5.8 Summary

- Find out what your audience wants before you start creating your intranet.

- The Home Page is the starting point of an intranet. It serves as a contents page, with text and icons providing links to the topics. Include a company name and logo on the Home Page and a brief description about the purpose of your intranet.

- A Home Page should be inviting and clear. Only include the main subject headings. Sub-headings can be included once the user has moved into the body of the intranet.

- Always include the date when the Home Page was last updated and a section on 'What's New' or 'Latest News'.

- Choose clear colour schemes for your pages and use these consistently to give a unified image to related items. White is a surprisingly popular and effective background.

- Try to break up long documents into different pages. Use HTML links to go to the next page rather than making the user scroll through large chunks of text.

5.9 Checklist

1 Survey your users to find out their general familiarity with computers and the idea of the intranet. This could influence the complexity, or otherwise, of the pages that you create.

2 Check all of your page links to make sure they work properly.

3 Do not get too carried away with your design. Keep it simple and effective.

4 Check pages with graphics or photographs to make sure they do not take too long to download.

5 Have a clear contrast between text colours and backgrounds.

6 Be consistent with text size and the use of capital letters.

7 Check pages to make sure that they have enough, but not too many, links to other parts of the system.

8 Contact some IT design consultants to see what they can offer in the way of intranet design.

6 | IMPLEMENTING AN INTRANET

6.1 Agreeing ownership

Who owns an intranet? This is the 64,000-megabyte question for any organisation that is thinking about installing an intranet system. Is it the management of the company? Is it the people who design and control the pages? Or is it the IT sections who ensure that the information keeps flowing through cyberspace? The answer is none of these. The real owners of an intranet are the people at the end of the line, the users. This should be displayed in large letters by anyone who has anything to do with the production, installation and maintenance of an intranet. If you lose sight of the fact that the users play a pivotal role in any intranet system then your project is doomed to failure.

So if the users own the intranet it seems only fair that they are consulted about it before it is created. There is little point in creating an intranet with what you *think* people will want, only to find that out after months of development and planning that you have been going down completely the wrong path.

You will need to conduct some market research to find out the type of intranet the users would like. Select a focus group of people in your organisation (covering all levels of experience and seniority) and send them a questionnaire. Ideally this could be done via e-mail, just to get them used to the idea of increased communication via computers. Tell them a bit about the concept of an intranet, ask them what they would like to see on it and how they would like to see the information presented, i.e. very simple and easy to use or something a little more sophisticated and streamlined.

6.2 Running a pilot study

Having been given the views of the prospective users, and acted upon them, you should set up a pilot group who will be able to use the intranet before it goes 'live' to the rest of the organisation. This should consist of at least 5% of employees, from different sections of the organisation and at different levels of seniority. It is important to have this range of users because you will get perspectives from throughout the organisation. Also, it will show the users in general that the intranet is for everyone, and everyone is equal in the eyes of the intranet.

Before you start a pilot study forget any preconceived ideas about what you think an intranet should be like or what you believe the pilot group will think of it. You may have been working so closely with the project that you could have missed some obvious points and these might be flagged up by the pilot users. Be prepared to listen to what the users say and adapt your system accordingly. If the majority of the users do not like something then change it, even if it is your favourite part of the system. This is the time to sit back, take notes and act on what the users are saying.

You should let your pilot study run for at least a month and preferably longer. This will allow the users to get a good feel for the system and it will also give the intranet editor a chance to operate the system as if it were 'live'. Give plenty of time and consideration to updates and adding new material: if the pilot users become bored quickly then you have little hope of impressing a wider audience. Try different methods of presenting new information (flashing it on the Home Page, scrolling it across the screen or having a *What's New* button) and see which one the users prefer.

At the end of the pilot study, ask each of the users to detail their experiences. Ask for a reasonable amount of coverage of all sections of the intranet, as well as specific items such as the Home Page and the hypertext links. Once you have the feedback from the pilot study you should write this into a report and present it to your managers who, hopefully, will sanction the project. Once the pilot has been concluded, and your recommendations accepted, a full implementation can be undertaken.

Once your intranet is ready to be implemented it is tempting to try and make it available to the whole organisation in a matter of days. This is only natural, because you want everyone to see the fruits of your labour and gain the benefits. However, this is doomed to failure, mainly due to constraints of time. Installing the software to run an intranet on a Personal Computer (PC), Apple Mac or UNIX workstation can take anything from a few minutes to over an hour. This depends on the type of machine and the way it is configured. In some cases it can be fairly quick, but there will invariably be the odd little glitch along the way and the installation process will take longer than anticipated. It is a bit like fixing the car or doing DIY – there is always one bolt that won't move or one vital tool that is missing.

6.3 Assessing technical requirements

Servers

The server is the engine-room of any intranet. It is a computer running the software programs where all of the files are stored and it is where the users will come, via their browsers, to access the pages of the intranet. In simple terms it is a large filing cabinet that is available to everyone in the organisation. The standard type of server is a high specification desktop computer that is capable of storing the necessary server software and the HTML files that make up the data in the intranet. To ensure that it can operate an intranet on a variety of computer operating systems (OS) the server should be capable of running on standard operating systems such as Windows, UNIX, Novell Netware or the Apple Mac OS.

Servers are like any piece of computer software: the more users that are connected to them then the slower they become. If your organisation has 1000 users connected to one server then the operation of retrieving intranet files may be relatively slow. It is a good idea to have an average of one server for every 100–200 users although this may vary according to the location of the users (the further away they are then the greater the need for additional servers) and whether a lot of users will be accessing the servers at the same time. One good thing about servers is that you do not have to worry too much about the dual pinnacles of the computing world: processing speed and Random Access Memory (RAM – the memory that the computer uses when it is performing operations). Since servers only have to do fairly basic tasks (generally fetching and carrying of files) the speed and RAM are not of vital importance. Having said that, you will want a system that has a high specification Pentium processor and at least 32 Megabytes (MB) of RAM.

Networks

Once you have a server in place you will need to give all of your users access to it. This is done through the creation of a Network Operating System (NOS) which is the system that links all of the computers in your Local Area Network (LAN) or Wide Area Network (WAN) to the central server. The chances are that your organisation will have some form of NOS in place already but if not, or if it needs to be upgraded, here are some of the choices available:

- **Windows NT** (although NT stands for New Technology the acronym is the accepted usage). This is the recognisable Windows format that is specifically designed for networks. It is cheap, relatively easy to install and, as you would expect from a Microsoft product, it is easy to find a wide range of tools and accessories that are compatible with it.

- **Novell Netware**. This is another operating system that is designed specifically with networks and the intranet in mind. It is a high quality product but it can be slightly complicated from a technical point of view.

- **Macintosh OS**. As with most of the Macintosh products this operating system is easy to install and use, but there are not as many additional products available as for some of the other operating systems.

- **UNIX**. This is one of the oldest operating system around which can be complicated and relatively expensive to install. On the plus side, it is a robust system that has stood the test of time. Its freeware equivalent, **LINUX**, is becoming increasingly accepted by organisations large and small.

The NOS that is chosen will influence the type of server that is used, as it obviously has to be compatible with the operating system. While this decision will invariably be taken by the IT department it is worthwhile having a general understanding about how these things work.

On top of this there are issues such as Transmission Control Protocol/ Internet Protocol (TCP/IP) which defines how the information is passed between separate computers and networks. Although this is something that only really needs to concern the computer experts, it is worthwhile knowing of its existence.

Computers for the users

The majority of intranet users will be viewing the system through a Personal Computer (PC), an Apple Mac or a workstation monitor that is linked to a network and not a stand-alone unit. If your organisation does not have any of these in place then you should have a serious rethink about installing an intranet. Although the prices of these machines are falling on an almost daily basis and it is possible to buy a high-spec machine from any high street retailer for under £1000, this is still a significant cost if you have to buy computers for all of your employees. If you do not have some form of computer network already in place then it would be unwise to spend this kind of money solely to produce an intranet. Of course if the computers were going to be bought anyway then this would be an ideal opportunity to implement an intranet at the same time.

For most organisations that already have a computer culture throughout the company, introducing an intranet may just mean upgrading a few machines. This will probably not be necessary for the intranet alone. However, once it is up and running then it may affect other programs if the machine is old and lacking in memory. It is worth buying the newest machines that your organisation can afford, particularly as the more that you buy the greater the discount that you may be able to negotiate. If you want to buy second-hand then try the classified advertisements of newspapers and computer magazines. There are also some retailers who specialise in second-hand equipment. Try not to buy anything too old – there are good bargains to be had for machines that are only 6 months or a year old. Second-hand machines are a good idea if you want to provide a group outlet for the intranet. This is where employees who do not have computers on their desks, use one shared machine to access the intranet. It is like using a computer in a library and while it is not an ideal situation it enables everyone in the organisation to have some access to the intranet.

6.4 Working with IT sections

If you mention the word 'intranet' to IT experts the chances are that their eyes will light up and they will start extolling the virtues of JavaScript, applets and Common Gateway Interfaces. While these can be important parts of an intranet they are by no means essential, as some in the IT world would have you believe. Always take the more technical claims of IT people with a pinch of salt – it may just be that they are trying to dazzle you with their grasp of the latest technology on the market. This is not to say that IT sections do not play a vital role in the development and running of an intranet because they do. But this role has to be specifically defined and everyone must know exactly what is expected of him or her.

The area in which IT staff are indispensable is in the technical side of running an intranet. This may seem like stating the obvious, but it should be accepted that this is an area in which the layman, or the intranet editor, should not interfere. Once a decision to produce an intranet has been taken the IT section should be left in peace to decide the following:

- The type of server that runs the intranet;
- How and where the HTML files are stored on the server;
- The method for transferring files to the server and from the server to the browsers;
- How the necessary software is installed on desktop computers and workstations.

This does not mean that the people in charge of the intranet's content should have no interest or knowledge of these matters – those producing the pages must know where graphics and other files are stored, so that they can identify them correctly in the HTML code. But it should be accepted that this is an IT area of expertise and the staff should not be told how to do their job. This would be similar to a waiter interfering in a chef's kitchen.

IT staff will also be able to produce HTML files to be included on the intranet and this is where it becomes a bit of a grey area as to who does what. For an intranet to be successful, the overall editorial control of what goes onto the system and how it looks should be in the hands of a non-IT person or group, preferably those who have a good knowledge of the organisation and the people in it. The main problem with IT staff controlling content and design is that they sometimes lose sight of the fact that not everyone has their knowledge of computing and computer systems. Intranets should be designed with the most non-computer literate people in mind and non-IT people are usually best at achieving this.

So it is important to establish with IT sections at an early stage exactly who does what: technical and installation for IT; production and design by an editorial group. However, this does not mean that the knowledge of the computer experts should be limited to servers and browsers. If someone has a good understanding of HTML programming then they should be encouraged to pass this on to the people who will be creating the pages. If there are circumstances where IT staff are producing the pages in HTML themselves then they should be given clear guidelines on what is expected and how the final product should look.

In an ideal world the relationship between the IT experts and the people controlling the content and design of the intranet should be a productive and harmonious one. Unfortunately, this is not always the case and it is inevitable that at some point both groups will feel that the other is stepping on their toes. In order to minimise conflict, which will inevitably hinder the progress of the intranet, a project team should be in place to resolve any disputes and make sure everyone is concentrating on their own task. As well as having IT and editorial members on the team there should also be at least two or three people from other parts of the organisation. This not only acts as a good public relations exercise for the promotion of the intranet; it also brings a fresh perspective to the proceedings. Sometimes the people who are very close to a project miss the obvious and it takes an outsider to bring things back on track by asking simple, but pertinent, questions. This is also a good way to resolve any disputes that arise while the intranet is being planned and installed.

6.5 Consistency of implementation

Since an intranet is an egalitarian form of communication there is no logical reason why one person, or section, should have access to the intranet before another. Obviously, logistics dictate that not everyone will have the intranet software installed at the same time, but it should be up to the people operating the intranet to decide how the installation programme will run.

The initial problem you will come up against is the type of person who believes that their elevated position demands that they have access to every new initiative before anyone else. This should be resisted if at all possible. Not only is it a form of workplace bullying, it could also jeopardise the credibility of your system. If the majority of staff see that the senior managers have access to the intranet before them then they may well conclude that it is little more than a management toy that has little relevance to the wider workforce. The best way to avoid your project being hi-jacked by senior management is to decide on your own implementation process and, if necessary, write a report justifying your methods.

6.6 The implementation programme

Despite everyone's best efforts, implementing an intranet will probably take longer than first anticipated. In theory it seems simple enough: put the system together, let people know about it and then install the necessary software and enjoy the benefits. But life in the workplace is never as easy as that and you will find that day-to-day factors such as workload, meetings, technical hitches and the occasional crisis will all conspire to delay the installation of an intranet. To be realistic, it is a good idea to think of a timescale in which you want your system to be up and running, and then double it. If the concept of an intranet is new to a lot of people then they may not have it at the top of their priority list of things to do. In time, of course, this may change.

Installing software

The most time consuming technical part of the implementation programme will be putting the software onto PC or workstations throughout your organisation. IT sections traditionally have numerous demands on their time and installing software may not be at the top of their list of priorities. For this reason the roll-out of the software will be a slow process and not everyone will have it at the same time. Indeed, there could be a gap of several months between the first person in your organisation going on-line with the intranet and the last one. Therefore you will have to think carefully about how you want the coverage of staff to proceed. There is a good argument for saying that it should start with the most junior workers in the organisation, as these are the ones that traditionally receive the least in the way of information and news.

A good compromise is to target specific sections and give everyone access to the system. This way there is no jealousy between different grades and it can be demonstrated that the system is not elitist. This is also easier for the IT section as they can target a whole area and they do not have to jump around from place to place, installing the browser software on isolated machines. Before you start any installation make sure you have a programme in place for the entire organisation and let people know about it. This way it is clear that there is a logical and realistic programme and no one is being favoured over someone else. Emphasise the fact that it is impractical for everyone to have the software installed at the same time.

Rolling-out the system

To make sure that your project does not get swamped under the weight of priority tasks that are increasingly common in most organisations today you should draw up an implementation programme for the roll-out of your intranet installation. The programme should be realistic (18 months from start to finish is not unreasonable when you consider all the other pressures that will be on everyone's time), genuinely achievable and with a specific target date for completion. If anything, be conservative with your estimates. If you achieve your targets before you anticipated then this will be seen as success but if you overrun then it will undermine confidence in the project.

The first part of your implementation programme should be to ensure you have enough information on the system to maintain interest. Contact all of the departments in your organisation, asking for input. Make sure that everyone knows that the intranet will evolve and grow from its initial version. Once you have done this then draw up a training programme. Do this through a simple database using all members of your organisation (personnel sections should be able to supply you with the relevant information). You can use the database to create a mailing list to send out to everyone telling them about the intranet and the training arrangements and then once the training is complete you can tick this off your master list. Keep a section for comments that people make when they reply – this may come in useful for including in the training courses.

Following installation

Once an entire area has access to the intranet they can begin using it. They should be informed of this officially, rather than just seeing a new icon appear on their computer one morning. Do this with a letter or, better, an e-mail. Let them know that the system is now operational and that you would welcome any comments, ideas or contributions.

Give staff regular updates about how the implementation programme is going. If progress is made consistently then those at the end of the list will have confidence that they will not be left out or forgotten about.

One important factor to consider with an implementation programme is that until everyone has equal access to the system you should not put anything on it that does not appear elsewhere in another form. For instance, do not put your office newsletter on the intranet and discontinue the hard copy to non-intranet users. This would limit access to those who have the intranet. This is a recipe for disaster as it creates two separate communication systems and the potential for confusion and conflict is huge. Until the implementation programme is completed, treat the intranet as a parallel system to those already in place. Once a section has the intranet then they can have hard copies of documents withdrawn but make sure they are still circulated to other parts of the organisation until they too have access to the intranet.

6.7 Back-up procedures

Although modern technology can do amazing things, and at times be a joy to work with, there are occasions when it all goes horribly wrong and the technology actually becomes an obstacle to getting anything done. This was illustrated in the United States when a faulty satellite caused most of the telephone pagers around the country to stop working. Even with the most efficient and well maintained IT system available there is always the possibility that, at some point in its lifespan, it will crash. If you are prepared for such an eventuality then at least you will have an emergency procedure to put into place.

Although it is not necessary for the intranet editor or the users to know how the system is backed-up, it is important that they know it is being done. This is an essential part of the maintenance of an intranet and one that could be invaluable to an organisation. In the worst case scenario of a fire destroying a company's entire premises, all of the information on the intranet could be retrieved if it has been backed-up and stored securely. This is not only a good insurance policy, it is also a major selling point when you are trying to convince your Managing Director to invest in an intranet.

The backing-up of IT data is usually done on magnetic tape and then it should be stored in a fireproof safe or container. However, the best solution is to have an off-site storage unit for backed-up material. It is good practice to back-up data everyday and the intranet editor should check with the IT department to ensure that this is what is happening.

Even though intranet technology is relatively straightforward and has proved to be fairly robust to date, you should have a contingency plan ready for the worst case scenario. In most organisations, this will be if all of the employees are connected to the intranet and there are no hard copies of anything circulating. If the intranet fails at this point then there is the potential for confusion, loss of production and downright annoyance. As part of your implementation programme you should also draw up a procedure for this possibility. Make sure that your users know what to do if the system fails – have an intranet hotline to telephone in case of emergency.

Identifying the essentials

The first task is to identify what is essential on the intranet. Obviously, you will consider everything to be important but daily notices and the telephone directory may be seen as more crucial than the latest training opportunities or the new issue of the staff magazine. Write down what you think are the priorities and then think of another way to distribute them to staff. One avenue to explore is having a network directory on a central server that everyone on the network can access. This would have to be separate from the intranet server and the users would only be able to access the information in their original form, e.g. word processing files, spreadsheet or desktop publishing files. IT personnel will be able to give you more information about the feasibility of using a shared directory.

If the worst comes to the worst and all of your computer systems fail (did anyone mention the Millennium Bug?) then you will have to turn to good, old-fashioned paper. Again you should identify what really needs to get to staff and treat this as a priority. Liaise with your printing or reprographics section and alert them to the urgency of the situation. It would be a good idea to create special Stop Press notices that can tell staff anything they need to know and also inform them about the situation with the intranet and the computer network. Each situation like this will be different in every organisation so you will need to use your initiative and hope that the technology is not disabled for too long.

6.8 Summary

- Before an intranet can be contemplated, an IT audit should be undertaken to find out what hardware and software your organisation possesses. Steps can then be taken to work out what would be needed to run an intranet. A minimum would be a server, PCs (or equivalent) and browsers.

- It should be clearly defined who does what between IT and communications sections. IT should deal with the technical aspects such as running and maintaining the server and the software while the communications staff should be in control of the style and the substance of the intranet.

- The owners of an intranet are those who use it. Concentrate on their requirements and try to look at the intranet from their perspective. Do not use it as a tool to promote your own agenda or score points against individuals or sections.

- Try and avoid creating a two-tier system of communication between those who have access to the intranet and those who do not. If some people do not have a computer, try and arrange for a 'shared' computer to be installed in their area. This could be a terminal that is used exclusively for the intranet.

- Be consistent when you installing the intranet. Do not begin by giving it only to the top management – carry out the installation by location rather than by seniority.

- The information on the intranet must be backed up regularly, in case of loss by theft, fire or hardware failure.

6.9 Checklist

1 Make a list of what hardware and software needs to be bought to run an intranet.

2 Put down on paper who is responsible for the various parts of the intranet – technical control, editorial control and overall control.

3 Let the users know that ultimately it is their intranet and they should play an active part in its development.

4 Draw up an implementation programme. This should be logically structured and have specific deadlines.

5 Promote the benefits of the intranet but be realistic. Do not let people think the intranet is going to radically change every aspect of their life.

6 Run a pilot study. Seek constructive feedback and act on it.

7 Base the intranet on what the users say, not what you believe.

7 | CAPTURING THE AUDIENCE

7.1 Training staff

If you have been involved in the planning, production and implementation of an intranet then you could be forgiven for thinking that it is the easiest, most straightforward computer system to use. You will be so familiar with its appearance and method of operation that you may feel that the users will have no problem in adapting to the intranet and they will welcome it with open arms. But stop for a few moments and ask yourself what you thought when you first saw the Internet or an intranet. Did you think, 'This looks like an effective and easy-to-use new communications tool', or did you shake you head, saying, 'What on earth are all of these buttons and different coloured pieces of text for?' Even if it was the former, it is more likely that your users will tend towards the second opinion. When introducing a new computer-based system you should always think of the least computer-literate people in your organisation.

With the almost ubiquitous inclusion of desktop computers into office and everyday life it is easy for people working with them to fall into the trap of thinking that they are easy to work with. It is true that modern computers and software packages have evolved into very sophisticated machines that offer huge potential for the business and personal user. But this does not mean that everyone exploits this potential. In the workplace, most people working with computers only use them to about 10% of their full capability. Despite the emergence of multimedia personal computers and the information superhighway, many people still have a distrust of new computer technology and, perhaps more importantly, they have a lack of knowledge of what this technology can do for them.

It is this combination of distrust and lack of knowledge that anyone introducing an intranet has to tackle. If you suddenly announce to the staff of your organisation that an intranet has been put in place, you will find that people will question your motivation for installing it and deluge you with queries about how to use it. What you have to do is train people in using the system and also convert them into accepting that an intranet will help them do their jobs more effectively. Training is the foundation on which any new initiative or process is built, and the intranet is no different to any other new system in this respect.

Organising effective training

In the present economic climate, employees in business and other organisations find that there are more and more demands being placed on their time at work. Everyone wants increased productivity, multi-tasking and the inevitable paperwork that even the computer age has not managed to remove. So when you are planning your training programme for the intranet you should bear in mind that you will be dealing with a lot of busy people who may think they have better things to do with their time than listen to you. What you have to do is convince them otherwise.

Your first step should be to alert staff to the general idea of the intranet. A notice or a one-page flyer that is circulated around the organisation can do this. Treat it like an advertising campaign and do not be afraid to sell yourself and your product. Keep things simple, stress the benefits and tell people that they will be shown how to use the system in the near future.

Once you have whetted everyone's appetite about the intranet you can devise a training strategy. If possible, this should be done in person to allow staff to ask questions on a one-to-one basis. You can either arrange for staff to come to a central point or you can have a mobile approach and visit different geographical locations in your organisation.

Your presentation should be short, factual and punchy. Start with a slideshow (either on an overhead projector or a laptop computer if the groups of people are small enough) covering the three basic facts that people will want to know:

- What it is
- What they can get out of it
- How to use it

Once you have gone over the basics, people will want to see an example of an intranet. Again, a laptop computer is useful for this as you can install some HTML pages and give a brief demonstration. If you have over a dozen people then you may need to project the pages onto a screen, but this will depend on what presentational equipment you have at your disposal.

Ideally, your training session should take no more than half an hour and then you can answer questions from your audience, who are, hopefully, wide-eyed with wonder by this stage. Once the session is over, give everyone a handout summarising what you have covered in your presentation. Make sure that you include step-by-step instructions about using an intranet and include a telephone contact number they can use if they have any questions or comments.

It is important that training only takes place once you have an installation programme in place: there is no point telling people about the advantages of an intranet if they have to then wait weeks or months until they see the real thing. If possible, give everyone at the training session a date that the intranet will appear on their desktop computers. If staff see that the system is being implemented in a serious and professional manner then they are more likely to be enthusiastic about it when they come to use it. Once the initial training has been given, and the users are using the system, the intranet can then be used as a training tool itself by putting on additional information on the training page. This could cover topics such as:

- A basic overview
- Creating pages in HTML
- Using interactive elements such as forms and questionnaires
- Guidelines for the corporate identity of the system

In addition, external training courses covering topics related to the intranet or Internet could also be placed on this site for people who want to learn more about the wired world.

7.2 Overcoming computer phobia

Just as some people have never come to love the car, so some people find it hard to embrace computer technology with open arms. They either believe they will never be able to master it or they think its existence threatens the very fabric of our society. Obviously this is something of a challenge for the champion of a new intranet system. Hopefully the training will go some way to solving the first problem, but the concept of computer phobia presents a different challenge.

Demonstrating simplicity

Not everyone likes the idea of using computers and very often this is rooted in a belief that they are difficult to use. In some cases this is definitely true, but as software technology improves so computers become more user-friendly, almost to the point where they can do the work for you and make a cup of tea in the process! Even if this is the case, it still has to be proved to the reluctant users. The only realistic way to do this is to sit them down at a computer and show them how easy it is to operate. Obviously, they will need some guidance, but one of the best ways to help people to learn is to show them the basics and then let them practise on their own. There is nothing worse than trying to come to terms with a new concept when there is someone staring over your shoulder. This is not to say that there should not be some advice on offer when needed, but keep a discreet distance. One thing worth stressing to a novice user is that, unless they have a particularly unique talent, there is very little serious damage that they can do to a computer or its programs.

In many ways the intranet is ideal for the reluctant users: it is easy to learn how to use it; the impact can be dramatic and it is impossible to delete or damage any files or pages. If you have a training facility where a spare terminal can be set up with the intranet then this would be ideal. Staff could come and try out the system at their leisure, thus gaining user experience and, hopefully, being more enthusiastic and confident when they see the real thing on their own computers.

Lessening the threat

The other reason people take a dislike to computers is that they see them as a threat to their jobs. While the prospect of massive job shedding due to increased usage of computers was slightly over-exaggerated in the early days of personal computers, it is a consideration when introducing a new computer-based communications system. In some areas, such as printing and distribution of documents, it is true that an intranet would probably have an impact to a greater or lesser degree. Whether this is likely to threaten jobs depends on the size of the company but if this is the case then it should be tackled head on. If the intranet is a very large one then there could be re-training opportunities to deal with the increased work in this area. Usually if the workload diminishes in one part of an organisation then it will increase proportionally in another area. Be aware of these issues, as you will want to avoid alienating any of your users if possible. In general, intranets should make people's jobs easier rather than redundant.

7.3 Encouraging active participation

The key elements in making any intranet work successfully are the users and how they react to it. If you have produced a professional, informative and easy-to-use site, you are off to a good start. Training and marketing should then be undertaken to let people know about it and how to use the system. But the real proof of success is whether users take an active interest in the system and accept it as an everyday business tool.

One surefire way of causing animosity or apathy towards an intranet, (aside from displaying inaccurate information), is to create a system that, in the eyes of the users, is for disseminating management propaganda. The system has to be viewed as an exciting and vibrant new technology that has at least a degree of editorial independence. To overcome this you should take every opportunity (when you are announcing the intranet for the first time, at training sessions and when you are implementing the system) to promote the fact that the intranet belongs to the employees and it is up to them to decide what goes on it. Of course, there are limitations to this, but highlight the role of the intranet editor as a genuine link between staff and management. If the users have confidence in the intranet editor, there is a good chance that they will have confidence in the system itself.

Generating excitement

People want easy access to high quality information from their intranet, but they also want to be excited by it – the 'wow factor'. Many people will not have seen anything like this, particularly in the workplace and even the simple function of linking from one page to another is likely to impress them. So make sure that the system is working properly before it goes live. Test all the links and make sure that the pages with graphics do not take too long to download – speed, or lack of it, kills as far as generating enthusiasm is concerned. Staff will want to feel they are experiencing something new and exciting. For instance, if you are putting your office newsletter on the intranet, create the on-line version in a different style to the paper copy. Do not just create screen versions of what you already have in the office. Be different and be innovative – the users will thank you for it.

Having, hopefully, won people over to the idea of the intranet you can begin to encourage them to take a more proactive role in its evolution. Have a 'Hotline' telephone number or, even better, an e-mail link on the intranet itself, for users to give their views and suggestions. Ask them what they think about the information on it and what additional material they would like to see. Take all of these views into account and act on them if at all possible. Even if you do not agree personally with all of the ideas or suggestions it is still worth implementing some of them. If the users feel that their views are being taken on board then this will increase their feeling of ownership of the intranet, which is one of the fundamental philosophies of a communications system of this type.

7.4 Overcoming the fear of the unknown

No matter how hard you market the intranet and how thorough your training programme is, there will always be some people in any organisation who are against the idea on principle. They dislike and distrust anything that is new or different and they adopt the attitude, 'It's always been done this way so why change?' This is the hardest group of people to win over because not only are they set in their ways but this also brings with it an ingrained cynicism and resistance.

In situations like this it is best to face the problem head-on and try to win over the cynics with the type of language they understand, money. If you can promote the intranet as a labour-saving, cost-cutting device and show how these costs could benefit everyone in the organisation then you are well on the way to winning over even the most hard-nosed cynics. Employees who are most resistant to change usually believe that restructuring and reorganisation is often done for the sake of it and they cannot see any tangible benefits that result from it. If you can demonstrate that the organisation can save X thousands of pounds a year and individuals can make their working day more productive then the cynics may be more willing to buy into the concept of an intranet. Do not be afraid to confront their reluctance and point out that the intranet is a system that can make a genuine and noticeable difference. If it contributes to the overall success of the organisation then everyone should feel more positive and motivated.

When you are making a case to convince the more sceptical members of your organisation be careful not to get too carried away. It is fine to promote the potential savings that can be made with an intranet but do not then claim that these savings will be passed on directly to the employees. How the savings are used is a management decision and all you can do is try and maximise these benefits and hope that the staff are treated generously.

7.5 Dealing with expectation and reality

Whatever your own personal hopes and expectations are for the intranet, it would be unwise to promote it to the users as being the best thing since the invention of the wheel. The simple reason for this is that if you implement it in a blaze of glory, making numerous exaggerated claims about its potential and the way it is going to revolutionise life in your organisation, then the chances are the reality will not live up to this and you will end up with egg on your face. More importantly, the intranet will be seen as a disappointment. By all means be positive and optimistic about the intranet and do not be afraid to promote its benefits. But err on the side of caution: if staff have modest expectations of the system they may find that they are pleasantly surprised by what it can do and how they can use it to their benefit.

Your own expectations for the system should be as high as possible and you should strive to make your intranet as big a success as you can. Be prepared to overcome some hurdles along the way because any new system has its problems. Do not become downhearted by these and always keep the bigger picture in mind. Even when things are going well you should be aware of potential pitfalls and let people know if you think there is going to be a problem. You should view the intranet as a long-term project and persuade the users to do the same. Tell them that it is not going to just be a 'one hit wonder' but in years to come it will be regarded more as a 'golden oldie'.

7.6 Summary

- Even though an intranet is relatively easy to use, people still need to be trained on how to get the most out of it. Not everyone in your organisation will be computer literate so keep it simple and do not go overboard with jargon or technical terminology.

- The intranet offers a number of benefits for individuals and organisations in terms of cost savings and the flow of information. However, in some circles these have been promoted to exaggerated levels. The intranet can be a very useful communications tool but it is not a magic wand.

- Some people will be hostile to the intranet because they just do not like computers. Be prepared for this and give them time to get used to the concept.

- The intranet is not a static medium. It needs to be used and used regularly. Encourage the staff to do this by keeping it up-to-date, visually attractive and by including interactive elements such as questionnaires and surveys.

- If people are reluctant to embrace the intranet at first, persevere. It should be seen as a long-term project. After using it for a while, people will begin to wonder how they ever did without an intranet.

7.7 Checklist

1 Make sure you have a training programme in place that includes everyone in your organisation.

2 Prepare a short and concise training presentation.

3 Arrange for an intranet demonstration as part of the training.

4 Do not be afraid to promote the benefits of the intranet, but be realistic.

5 Acknowledge the fact that some people just do not like PCs and will have to be won over.

6 Ensure people are willing and able to actively use the intranet.

7 Have an emergency plan in place in case the gremlins turn your computer system into little more than a collection of flashing lights and error messages.

8 Keep your ear to the ground to find out what people are saying about the intranet – never under-estimate the power of gossip or office politics.

8 | MANAGING AN INTRANET

8.1 Searching the intranet

When you first develop your intranet it may only have a dozen or so sites and a hundred or so pages of information. This will make it relatively easy and straightforward to navigate around and users should not have too much trouble finding the information that they are looking for. However, since the intranet is, or should be, a constantly evolving medium, this state of affairs is unlikely to continue for very long. As more people use the intranet then there will be an increased number of requests for items to be placed on it. Before you know it, the content will have grown dramatically. Some intranets have thousands of pages of information and it is not uncommon to find intranets with over a million pages on them. This obviously presents a challenge to whoever is managing the system. One option is to leave the users to their own devices and let them trawl through pages and pages of information before they stumble across the item they are looking for. Understandably this will leave them frustrated, annoyed and unwilling to repeat the whole process in a hurry. Alternatively you could install a sophisticated search facility on your system to allow users to find information quickly and easily.

Although a good search facility is vital to the professional management of an intranet it should not be used as a shortcut for other ways of making information easily accessible to users. Before inviting people to dive into a search tool you should make sure that you have the following items in place.

Contents list

There must be a thorough and comprehensive list of contents on your Home Page. This may seem like common sense, but when you are regularly putting new pages onto the system it is easy to forget about updating the

Home Page. (There are programs that can monitor links to check that they are all current.) It is essential to list all of the main areas on your intranet and these sections should then have their own detailed list of contents. You should review your list of contents regularly to make sure it is up-to-date and accurate. Ideally, users should only have to make three or four mouse clicks to get to the item they are looking for.

Bookmarks or Favorites

These are the names used by the browsers (Bookmarks for Netscape Navigator and Favorites for Microsoft Explorer) for the function of noting which pages you visit most frequently. You can add your favourite pages to this and it is a useful shortcut if you know what files you want to access. However, it is only of use if you know what you are looking for.

The use of keywords

Whenever you create a document you can attach a list of keywords to it, to help a search facility look for it. (This is how search engines on the Internet work: you give them a list of keywords and then the users will hopefully enter the same keywords when they are looking for the document.) Keywords should be simple and relevant to the document, and keep in mind the fact that people searching for a document may not associate the same words with it as you do.

What is a search engine?

Designed originally to sift through the massive volume of information on the Internet, search engines are software devices that look through lists of words, filenames and directories to try and find matches for a specific enquiry. As anyone who has used the Internet knows, this can often lead to thousands of possible matches, some of which are irrelevant or just plain daft. The secret to utilising a search engine effectively is in the keywords that are attached to the documents to be searched and also the criteria selected for the search. Search engines are very sophisticated and can search for subjects, individual words, filenames and even images. The secret is in the indexing: when you create documents take the time to add keywords to them. This is done through the Document Properties or Properties menu used in most applications. For instance, in Microsoft Word you can select Properties from the File menu and then add any relevant keywords in the subsequent dialogue box.

When you first use them, search engines can be frustrating because you are invariably given so many possibilities that you are not much further forward with your search than when you started. This is due to the lack of sophistication of the initial query. If you search an intranet for the word 'staff' then you will probably register a large number of related items. However, if you refine this to 'sales staff', the number will be considerably reduced. Search engines also include facilities so that you can widen your search, eliminate certain words or find closely related topics. This is usually done with the use of the words AND, OR, NOT and NEAR. The more that you use a search engine the more sophisticated you will become with your searching techniques. With practice you will gain a good understanding of what works for you and your system. A good way to see what search engines have to offer is to use one on the Internet. These display most of the latest searching techniques and are useful for seeing what the capabilities of these tools are. Some popular Internet search engines are:

Yahoo   http://www.yahoo.com/

AltaVista   http:www.altavista.digital.com/

Excite   http://www.excite.com/

There are several search tools on the market and it is best to look for one that has been designed with the intranet specifically in mind. Some of those available include:

- **Verity SEARCH '97**. More information about SEARCH '97 can be found on the Internet at **http://www.verity.com/**

- **CompassWare InfoMagnet**. This is a sophisticated search engine that uses a wide range of query devices and also employs filters to allow for a more specific search. More information about InfoMagnet can be found on the Internet at **http://www.compassware.com/**

- **Adobe Acrobat Search**. More information about Acrobat Search can be found at **http://www.adobe.com/**

- **Quarterdeck WebCompass**. Another sophisticated search engine and one that is particularly useful for large intranets that are constantly having information added to them. More information about WebCompass can be found on the Internet at **http://www.quarterdeck.com/**

8.2 Maintaining interest

An intranet should be looked at as a long-term project and not something to be developed and then left to gather dust on a computer server. One of the most common reasons for an intranet to fail is that it is not maintained and updated properly and so the users quickly become disillusioned and stop logging-on. It is not unrealistic to say that an intranet should be updated and added to on a daily basis – imagine a newspaper that carried exactly the same information for several days, or even weeks, running. It is essential to the long-term well being of an intranet that suitable human resources are made available to ensure that it is an evolving medium rather than a static one.

Adding new items

In most organisations there is something newsworthy that happens every day. This may be in the form of a general notice, staff information, social news or company news. Whatever it is, it should be put on the intranet. People like seeing new information and they begin to value a source that can give it to them quickly. The intranet has the advantage over paper-based communications in that it does not have to be printed and then distributed manually. The intranet can give people the latest news almost immediately and it should be used to do this. If users accept it as the definitive medium for providing new information then it will have gone a long way to gaining widespread acceptance.

Date stamps

Whenever new items are placed on the intranet they should be marked with the date and time that they were published. This not only lets the users see when they first appeared but can also galvanise the intranet editor into making sure that there is always something new to replace outdated items.

However, once users have become accustomed to the intranet as their main provider of news and up-to-date information you then have to make sure this is rigorously maintained: if there is a break in the flow of communication then doubts will creep in about the reliability of the system.

There should be a timetable drawn up detailing what type of information is placed on the intranet and at what times. This could include some of the following information:

- Daily: Notices, staff news, urgent developments.
- Weekly: Company information, product updates, updated telephone lists, staff moves.
- Monthly: Publications, such as newsletters, briefings, production reports.

With the exception of earthquakes or freak tidal waves, this timetable should be adhered to strictly. Make sure that there is backup of at least three people who can implement this timetable if the intranet editor (or editorial team) is indisposed. It is impossible to over-stress the importance of consistent and regular updates to an intranet: without them the system will wither and die, amid a welter of recriminations and disappointment.

Updating existing information

As well as constantly adding new information to your intranet you will also need to be aware of existing items and whether they are still up-to-date or not. It is easy to forget about files that are already on the system and concentrate instead on new items that may seem more exciting and interesting. However, if you do this then you are in danger of creating an intranet that quickly becomes stale and dated. If all pages have a creation date on them (as they should) then it is easy for users to see how long a particular piece of information has been on the system. This is okay if the information does not change but if there is updated data that can be included then you should make every effort to do so. If you do not, then you can guarantee that someone will notice it and point it out to you. This makes the intranet look amateurish and less than thorough.

To keep a track of the files and pages that may need to be updated you should create a database of all of these files, listing which ones should be reviewed daily, weekly, monthly or even yearly. As part of your maintenance of the system make sure that you look at the database regularly and mark off what checks have been done. Another way to revise pages is to ask the users to alert you to new information or data that has been changed. If you approach it in this way then the users will think that you are proactive rather than absent-minded.

Deleting old information

As with even the tidiest house there comes a time when any intranet needs a good, old fashioned spring-clean. Inevitably there will be a collection of redundant, irrelevant or just plain old files on the system. It is the job of whoever is in charge of content to decide whether these files need to be kept or if they could be deleted from the system. When considering what should stay or what should go, the following criteria can be followed:

- Does the information serve a specific purpose?
- Is the information accessed and used regularly?
- Will there be a wailing and a gnashing of teeth if it were removed?

If the answers to the above are NO then you can probably take the items off the system with impunity. If it is being kept because of the 'What if' philosophy? (i.e. keeping something on the remote chance that it might, one day, be useful) then it would also be fairly safe to remove it. If you want, some information could be taken off and stored on tape. This way it could be kept as an archive for as long as it might be needed.

The main advantage of cleaning up your intranet is that it makes it more streamlined for the users and takes up less disk space on the server. In order to keep your intranet fresh and vibrant you should draw up a 'spring-cleaning' rota, at least once every three months, and stick to it. The users will certainly thank you for it.

8.3 Site management

The worst thing to do to an intranet is to leave it unattended. This is like running a high-performance engine without any oil: before too long it will seize up and grind to a halt. The same is true of an intranet. It needs daily maintenance to ensure that it keeps running smoothly and this is known as site management.

The concept of site management refers to the overall operation of the intranet. It is concerned with the way that all the files on the system relate to one another and whether the links throughout the system are maintained and functioning properly. Links can be broken easily by changing file names, moving files or accidentally deleting files that are

still operating as a live link. It is the job of site management to identify
these problems when they occur and mend the broken links. Site
management can also undertake global changes to parts, or all, of the
intranet, such as changing the structure and design of specific pages. For
instance, if you wanted to change the background colour of a group of
pages this could be achieved through one command using a site
management tool.

Although some aspects of site management could theoretically be
undertaken manually, it would be a Herculean task involving large
databases of filenames and relevant links. The work involved would limit
the actual time developing the intranet; which is why site management
software was invented.

Managing your site with software

Intranet site management packages usually go hand-in-hand with the
related page-authoring tool and it is best to use the two together. So the
Adobe PageMill authoring tool works most effectively with the Adobe
SiteMill site management package, as does Microsoft's FrontPage Editor
for authoring and FrontPage Explorer for management. The basic
functions that a site management package will perform are:

- A general overview of what you have on your intranet. This
  can include directories, folders, files, pages and images.
- An alert facility to let you know when there are missing links.
- Restoring broken links and ensuring that the user does not
  reach a dead-end.

As with page authoring tools, there are a number of site management
packages on the market and these include:

- Microsoft FrontPage Explorer (present in the full FrontPage
  package, but not in FrontPage Express).
- NetObjects Fusion.
- Adobe SiteMill.

Whatever site management tool you choose you should use it frequently
to check that the files and the links on your intranet are doing their job
and creating a continuous chain through the system. If possible, include
this on your list of daily tasks.

8.4 Ensuring security

Whenever computer systems and business are mentioned in the same sentence the question of security usually occurs shortly afterwards. The fundamental problem is that businesses are fearful that anything they put on a computer system such as an intranet could be accessed and corrupted by an external hacker (someone who specialises in breaking into supposedly secure computer networks). Hackers generally fall into three groups: computer buffs who see it as a challenge to break into the most high-profile computer networks they can find (such as NASA or the American Federal Reserve Bank); professional computer experts who hack into an organisation's network at their request in order to test their security measures; and individuals or groups who are intent on gaining access to networks for destructive purposes. Of the three, the first group usually comprises of teenagers who are only interested in the thrill of cracking the system; the second are dealt with later in this chapter; and the third are the ones who are of real concern to the business world. The thought that an organisation's data can be accessed, changed, deleted or added to by an external source is enough to send any chief executive into a cold sweat. There are two ways to try and limit the chances of this happening (although it would be a supreme optimist or a fool who claimed that any computer network was one hundred per cent secure). The first is to install a security device called a firewall at the point where your information can be accessed externally and the second is to invite someone to deliberately try and hack into your system so that potential weak spots can be identified.

Firewalls

A firewall is a piece of software that blocks unauthorised access to an organisation's intranet from external sources, most notably the Internet. It can operate as a straightforward barrier or it can be a separate location that stores incoming information to keep it away from the intranet. Its purpose is to monitor every file entering or leaving the Local Area Network so that it can detect any problems that might enter the network from unauthorised sources.

If your intranet does not currently have an external outlet you should keep firewalls in mind because sooner or later you will probably want to have an Internet connection via your intranet. There are two reasons for this: firstly to enable employees to use the Internet as a research tool and an outlet for external e-mails; and secondly so that certain information on your intranet can be made available to the general public. The latter can be useful if you want to advertise something such as your latest product information. If this is the case then this information should be placed on a separate server, which is the only part of the intranet that can be accessed via the Internet.

If, or rather when, you have a connection to the Internet this is where the fun begins. Not only can hackers worm their way into your intranet, gaining access to your corporate information, but there are also thousands of computer viruses that could be transmitted into your network via the Internet. Although many of these only constitute nuisance value there are some that can cause real damage by corrupting files and your operating system. This is where firewalls come into their own. They sit between the intranet and the Internet and check everything that wants to enter your system. Figure 8.1 illustrates the role of firewalls.

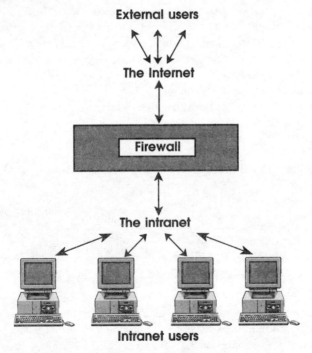

Figure 8.1 Example of how a firewall works

There are three main types of firewalls:

- The first type acts like a customs official, but instead of checking passports and visas it monitors the source and address of where the information has come from. The user has to specify what type of information they want to allow to enter via the Internet and if it does not match your requirements then it is refused entry.

- The second type operates by only allowing data from certain types of applications to enter the system. Again, you can specify which applications are acceptable and which are not.

- The third type is one that acts as a proxy between the intranet and the Internet. It sits between the two and stores all incoming information so that it is never directly in contact with the intranet.

Firewalls are usually the domain of the IT department and they can be made from scratch or bought off the shelf. Two points worth considering are that firewalls are only as secure as the way they are configured, i.e. you have to tell them exactly what you want them to do; and they do tend to slow down performance in return for improved security. In addition, firewalls must be upgraded regularly because new viruses are being developed continually and hackers are learning new tricks on a daily basis.

Tiger Attack teams

Tiger Attacks is the name given to the acceptable face of computer hacking. They are conducted by teams of computer experts who are invited by an organisation to try and infiltrate a specific computer network. They do this by using the latest IT technology and up to a dozen people work together to try to break into the system. Invariably they succeed in obtaining varying degrees of infiltration and they are then able to highlight the weaknesses in the system. This is an extreme way of checking how secure, or otherwise, your computer network is, but if you are worried about any aspect of security then it is worth looking into. Generally, the bigger the computer network then the greater the chances of finding weak links in its security.

Companies who perform Tiger Attacks are most firmly established in America but IT consultants around the world will also be able to perform this type of service. To locate consultants who undertake this type of work, search the Internet (try searching under *hackers*, *IT security*, *IT consultants* and *tiger team hackers*) to see which companies are advertising their services. Location or distance should not be a problem because this type of work can be carried out through the use of phonelines and computers, without the need for face-to-face meetings.

8.5 Avoiding information overload

One of the hardest aspects of managing an intranet is restraining yourself from overdosing on your new gizmo and loading every available piece of information onto the system. The temptation to do this is great, and understandable. Having planned and implemented an intranet you will be fully aware of its potential and want to share this with everyone in your organisation. However, if you go down the route of publishing huge swathes of information in a very short time you may find your audience is overwhelmed and they may feel threatened by the sheer volume of data that is being targeted at them.

Initially your intranet should have a modest amount of information on it. Enough to make it useful and not too much so that it becomes inaccessible. Once the users feel comfortable with the initial concept (and it is the very idea of an intranet that they will have to get used to rather than the actual data that is on it) then you can start building up the range and number of pages that you have on the system. This should not be done in one large wave of items, but rather with a steady flow of information. This way the users will still feel comfortable with the idea and they will be impressed if it is built up steadily and consistently. Do not rush the users; even if you are confident that they would be able to cope with a rapidly expanding intranet you should still take your time and let them get used the system. A lot of people are inherently suspicious of new forms of technology so let them get to know the intranet and befriend it.

Another consideration is the quality of the data that you put on the intranet. Information should not automatically be transferred en bloc onto the intranet. People do not assimilate text on screen as well as they do with hard copies so a certain degree of finesse is required when you are transferring paper-based material onto the intranet. In some cases this may mean editing certain documents so that they are in a form that is more easily digestible on the intranet. Do not be afraid to do this: as long as you do not change the meaning of an article or document then it is perfectly reasonable, and in some cases preferable, to have a different version for the intranet.

8.6 Summary

- Even though an intranet may start from humble beginnings the chances are that it will quickly grow into a large and diverse network of information. In order to let the users grow with the system you will have to provide a facility to find items on the intranet quickly and easily. There are a number of search tools available to perform these tasks.

- It is impossible for one person to keep track of all the files and links that are on an intranet so don't even try. Use a site management tool to keep your files and links working smoothly together.

- If users think your intranet is static, out-of-date or badly maintained they will quickly lose interest and log-off. Ensure that there is a steady stream of new information being put on the system and that existing pages are regularly reviewed for revising or deleting.

- No intranet is 100% secure. If, as is likely, your intranet is linked to the Internet then you run the risk of an attack from hackers. This may just be cyberspace high jinks or it could a genuine threat to your computer network and the information on it. Set up firewalls to prevent unauthorised access and invite professional hackers to try and get into your system in order to identify weak spots.

- If new users to an intranet are faced with a huge list of contents and thousands of pages of information they may run screaming from their computers, never to return. So as not to intimidate people, start small and build up from there. Add information consistently rather than large amounts in one go. Always look at documents in relation to how they will appear on the intranet and do not be afraid to amend them accordingly.

8.7 Checklist

1 Try out various search tools to see which one is the best for your uses. There are numerous examples of these on the Internet.

2 Make sure you have a programme in place for adding, revising and deleting information on the intranet. And stick to it.

3 If your intranet has a link to an external source, such as the Internet, then make sure there is a firewall in place.

4 Always presume that your intranet has security weak spots. If you are in doubt, invite IT consultants to try and break into your system.

5 Be selective about what you convert to the intranet. Quality wins over quantity every time.

9 | MAKING IT A SUCCESS

9.1 Keeping it simple

In order to make an intranet a success you will need to have people using it, and using it on a regular basis. To achieve this you will need to convince them that it is a simple and effective concept. The second part may be easy enough but the first part may come up against a bit more resistance. If you mention things like computer systems and anything computer related ending with the word 'net' then most people take on a glazed look as their mind fills with images of supergeeks and alien looking pieces of electronics. This is perfectly acceptable and the first thing that an intranet planner has to do is to convince the users that they do not need to know how an intranet works, only that it does. Just as a lot of people are blissfully ignorant of what goes on under the bonnet of a car, so most computer users do not have the slightest bit of interest in what goes on behind the screen. As long as it goes beep and springs into life when they press the ON button they are perfectly satisfied.

The best way to win over the users to an intranet is to mention computers and computer related terms as little as possible (particularly the numerous abbreviations and acronyms so beloved by computer boffins). They do not have to know of the intricacies of HTML, or the fact that it even exists at all; JavaScript and web authoring packages will leave them cold: information on file protocols will have them reaching for the OFF button in their droves; and the less said about motherboards, interfaces and firewalls the better. It may be tempting to dazzle the users with your knowledge of the intranet and what makes it tick but if you do then you may find that your system is only being used by a few computer buffs who actually know what you are talking about. Keep jargon and computer-speak to a minimum and let the intranet in all its simplicity do the talking.

9.2 Achieving empowerment

In the ever-changing world of management terminology and philosophy
the idea of empowerment is one that has become increasingly popular in
the 1980s and 1990s. Despite its rise to prominence in the business
vocabulary its true meaning is often misunderstood. To many employees
it means giving them the power to do what they think is best for them and
the organisation. In reality it should mean giving employees the power to
do their jobs to the management's specifications. This is a subtle difference
but an important one: in both cases the employees are given more
information but it is how they use this information that is important.
Through its ability to not only provide specific information but also show
how to use it, the intranet is a powerful tool in ensuring that employees
really are empowered to do their jobs for the increased benefit of the
organisation.

Giving people what they want

The first step to empowerment in the workplace is to give employees
what they want, or at least what they need, to do their jobs more effectively.
The intranet is an ideal medium through which to achieve this. Not only
can employees be given fundamental information such as telephone
directories, manuals and handbooks; they can also receive items that are
directly relevant to their jobs. By encouraging people to share ideas and
initiatives on the intranet a greater number of users will have information
which can be applied to their own situations. To make this truly effective
the information that is placed on the intranet should be relevant, accurate
and meaningful. If it is not, then it just wastes everyone's time and becomes
counter-productive.

It is the job of the intranet editorial committee to decide what should and
should not go onto the system. In this role they should act with the
organisation's best interests at heart, rather than what they think might
be best for the intranet. For instance, if a dynamic looking page is presented
for inclusion on the intranet but it has very little relevance to the work of
the organisation then it should be rejected, even if it would improve the
image of the intranet. The Internet can afford to include pages on a whim,
or because they look impressive but the intranet cannot. For this reason
the intranet editorial committee require a very good understanding of the
work of the organisation.

Every item should be subjected to the following questions:

- Will it help the organisation's employees to do their jobs more effectively?
- Is it in line with the overall business aims of the organisation?
- Will it lead to a tangible business benefit?

If the answer is 'yes' to all these questions, then it can make its way into cyberspace. If the answer is 'no' to any of them, then it is back to the drawing board.

In Chapter 6 it was shown that the users own the intranet. While this is true, it is not solely for their benefit; it is for the benefit of everyone in the organisation, from the managing director or chief executive down. So, ideally, if the intranet is a success then the employees can do their jobs more effectively, the organisation becomes more productive and the management view the whole project as a success. What happens then is up to the management but it shows that the intranet can play a vital part in promoting efficiency and productivity. That is what empowering employees is all about: giving them what they need, rather than just what they want. While in some instances these are the same thing, there will be times when you may have to look at something that people want on the intranet and conclude that it is not in the best interests of the organisation.

9.3 The communications strategy

So, you have created your intranet, it is up and running, the users are happily logging-on and receiving relevant and up-to-date information and everyone is happy. Well, not necessarily. What happens when someone from senior management turns around and asks, 'What are we getting for our investment in the intranet?' The obvious answer would be reduced costs, a better flow of information around the organisation, a more informed workforce and improved customer relations. Admittedly some of these may take a period of time to filter through the system and, if there is cost-cutting in the air, then the intranet may seem like a prime candidate for the axe to those who do not fully appreciate the value of this new technology. No matter how committed you are to the project, and how convinced you are of its worth, this may count for nothing if the bean counters feel it is not pulling its weight.

One way of insulating the intranet from the force of the corporate cost-cutting axe is to incorporate it into a long-term internal communications strategy. This has two advantages:

1 It clearly defines the intranet as a communications tool.
2 It shows that the intranet is integrated into the overall performance of the organisation.

A communications strategy should cover a wide range of communication mediums, all of which collectively contribute to the employees having a better understanding of what is going on both inside and outside the organisation. This in turn leads to increased productivity, better staff morale and improved customer service, all of which would please even the most churlish executive. A communications strategy is made up a number of different strands and some of these can include:

- Team meetings
- Workshops and seminars
- Information notices and bulletins
- Publications
- Training
- Electronic communication

All of these serve a specific purpose in informing and educating employees. So for the intranet to holds its own in a communications strategy, it has to be shown that it too can perform these functions. Therefore an intranet needs to be promoted as an improvement on existing methods of communication. If an intranet is presented to an executive as a simple one-for-one swap for paper-based forms of communication, he may very well ask why he should bother investing time and money in it. When an intranet is being created, it is important to look at the information that is being put on it and assess how the new system will be an improvement on the existing one. This can be shown in terms of:

- Cost savings
- Improved quality of information being presented
- Improved method of presentation and dissemination

Although the odds are stacked firmly in favour of the intranet over paper-based forms of communication it is dangerous to become complacent and over-confident. Always keep at the forefront of your thinking the fact that the intranet's main purpose (or sole purpose) is to make your organisation more successful. If you include it in an overall communication strategy, and show that it is more efficient than the systems already in place, then you should have few problems in persuading the powers that be to accept it as an everyday part of the organisation. Taking this one step further, if you list the savings and advantages of the intranet as you go along then you will soon have enough ammunition to show that the system is indispensable.

9.4 Devolving authoring responsibility

Sooner or later the people who are in charge of an intranet will have to decide whether they are to continue to be the sole means for authoring pages for the system, or if they should allow other users, sections and divisions to create their own pages. There are a number of reasons why this is a good idea:

- If you want to create a diverse and comprehensive intranet it would not be feasible for one person, or one group, to create all of the pages on their own.
- It is good to see what ideas other people have and what use they can make of the intranet.
- Users in different parts of the organisation will have a better idea of what is happening in their own areas and so they can create pages that are relevant and accurate. If an outside source were to do this then it would take them longer as they would have to do a certain amount of research on the area involved.
- If more people are included in the creation of pages then they will feel a greater loyalty to the system and they will actively promote it among their colleagues.

The downside to giving greater creative control to other people is that you may create a creature that begins to take on a life of its own. This does not have to be a disadvantage though. If there is still central editorial control then this could give a new impetus and vitality to the intranet. Managing an intranet is a bit like bringing up a child: sooner or later you will have to relinquish a little bit of control, no matter how hard it may seem at first.

When users are involved in creating their own pages, it is vital that they are given adequate training and guidelines to follow, and also that there is a central point that maintains overall editorial control. Training should be given in the creation of HTML files and also in the use of a web-authoring package. It is probably preferable if the latter is used so that the author can begin creating pages quickly and effectively. There is no need for them to have an intimate knowledge of HTML, unless they specifically show an interest in it. An HTML training facility could be included on the intranet itself to help users who want to try a bit of web authoring. However, this would mean that everyone would be aware of this possibility and you would have to decide if this is a desirable situation. It is important to do the training as thoroughly as possible, because if you cut corners then you will only create more work for yourself in the long-run, in terms of repairing other people's mistakes.

Guidelines for users who are going to be creating their own pages, are vital to maintaining the overall style and format of the intranet and also for keeping consistent styles for filenames and the use of links. Guidelines should includ the following information:

- The use of typefaces.
- The use of the organisation's name and its logo.
- The use of background colours and textures.
- The importance of using graphics and photographs carefully.
- The preferable length of documents and how well they will translate to screen.
- The number of links used and how they connect to various parts of the intranet.
- The need for maintaining, updating and revising any new pages.
- The importance of making sure that the information is accurate.
- A contact name, telephone number and e-mail address for issues regarding content, and one for technical issues.

You should also consider creating standard templates that users can copy to form the basis of their own HTML pages. This will help to ensure consistent styles, colours and typefaces.

As far as control over the content is concerned it is worthwhile having a definite structure in place for who does what. This could include:

- The overall intranet editor, or editors, should have the final say about whether a page is placed on the system.
- Each area creating their own pages should have a manager who decides what material is going to be put forward for inclusion on the system.
- Within the area there should be at least two or three people whose job it is to find the information and produce it in HTML format.

The creation of intranet pages can be looked at in the same way as the production of a newsletter or magazine would be: there are writers who pass articles to sub-editors to be checked, who then subsequently pass them to editors for final approval. This should be the case with the intranet too; if something appears on the system that is a shock or a surprise to the users then there has been a lapse somewhere in the chain of editorial communication. If in doubt, check with the people who have created the information and also the manager who is responsible for it.

9.5 Harnessing the Internet

Although intranets can operate independently from the Internet, there are distinct advantages for an organisation in having a connection to the Internet as well as running an internal intranet. The two main benefits are:

1 Using the Internet to develop and improve the workings of the intranet.
2 Using the Internet to stimulate business, which can then be cultivated via the intranet.

Using the Internet in conjunction with an intranet is also another positive factor as far as the users are concerned. It gives them another communications tool to use and helps to make them feel that they are part of a bigger, global, communications network.

Developing from the Internet

Anyone developing an intranet will need to keep up with the latest developments in design and technology. This is where the Internet comes into its own. Since it evolved from the self-same technology as used by intranets, there are literally thousands of web sites devoted to all aspects of Internet/intranet development. Since this type of technology is changing and improving almost on a daily basis, it is vital for an intranet designer to keep up with the latest trends. Some of the areas that should be monitored regularly are:

- **Browsers**: new versions always have additional features and can display a greater range of multimedia effects.

- **Servers**: greater speed and memory are the order of the day for each new generation of servers.

- **Firewalls**: it is important to keep up with the latest developments in IT security because you can be sure that the hackers are doing just that.

- **Software**: there is a mind-boggling array of software to be found on the Internet, ranging from animation programs to video conferencing packages. A lot of it can be downloaded free of charge or else there will be a demonstration version designed to show what the full program can do.

The one irritation when looking for information on the Internet can be the search process itself. For every useful piece of information you find you may have to plough through a dozen irrelevant items that are frequently only thinly disguised advertisements. A good way to start is to enter *intranet* into one of the search engines (Yahoo is a particularly effective one) and then add more words to the search criteria after each result is displayed.

Another useful option is to search the sites of some of the major computer companies in the world, such as Microsoft, Novell, IBM, Hewlett Packard, Sun Microsystems or Apple. Each of these companies has an extensive site, covering a wide range of computer related topics. Included in this will be information relating to intranet technology and the latest products on the market. Their web sites are:

http://www.microsoft.com/
http://www.novell.com/
http://www.ibm.com/

http://www.hewlett-packard.com/
http://www.sun.com/
http://www.apple.com/

The Internet is not only useful for finding out about the latest developments in technology but also for seeing what web designers are currently producing. This will probably consist of the good, the bad and the atrocious, and you will be able to pick up ideas about what to put on your pages, as well as what to avoid. If you see a design that you particularly like you can check how it was created by looking at the source HTML document on the browser. (**View, Source** on Internet Explorer and **View, Document Source** on Navigator). The items worth paying particular attention to are:

- Graphics
- Backgrounds
- Frames
- Tables
- Animations
- Multimedia effects
- Interactive devices

A list of useful Internet sites, covering everything from obtaining images to long-term intranet development, can be found in the further information section at the end of the book.

Marketing on the Internet

As well as using the Internet to pick up hints for developing an intranet, it can also be used as a marketing tool to promote your organisation. You only have to have a quick surf around the Internet to see that huge numbers of organisations, from all walks of life, have already realised the potential of self-promotion in cyberspace. It is a lot easier to obtain a presence on the Internet than many people think. Most Internet Service Providers (ISPs — organisations who provide you with the connection to the Internet) include the facility to create your own site and place it on the World Wide Web. If you have already designed an intranet then this should not be too much of a problem. Alternatively, there are numerous companies who design Internet sites, including the installation and maintenance of the finished product. Obviously, this is more expensive than adopting the do-it-yourself approach.

When you are creating an Internet site it is best to resist the temptation to make it a mirror image of your intranet. Despite the fact that they are both based on the same technology your internal and external sites will be performing two very different functions. The intranet will be providing specific, factual information aimed at people who are actively seeking it to do their jobs more effectively. The Internet site will perform the task of attracting people's attention to your organisation and whetting their appetite enough so that they want to find out more. To do this your Internet site should be designed along the following lines:

- Bold, eye-catching images
- Positive, dynamic statements
- Devoid of large chunks of unbroken text, or technical data
- Limited to generalities and not giving away any trade secrets

Since your prospective clients will be confronted by similar information from other organisations, your web page will need to catch their attention instantly and retain it for as long as possible. Give them an overview of your organisation in broad brushstrokes and tell them where they can find out more if they are interested. If you want to give out information about new products or your company's services then this can be done through pages linked to your Home Page.

If the Internet site does its job and the customer/client approaches your organisation, then this is where the intranet can come into the picture. With the use of firewalls you can allow external users access to sections of your intranet. This device is known as an extranet and it can be used to display information that is more specific than you may want to display on an Internet site. This way you can be sure that the visitors to your network are genuinely interested in your organisation and its work. The advantage of this is that it enables the customers to interact more with individual organisations, so building up better working relationships.

9.6 Ensuring long-term benefits

When the intranet first bursts onto the scene within your organisation it may be welcomed like an enticing looking gift box at Christmas: full of potential excitement but also containing the possibility of eventual boredom and disillusionment. In order to maintain interest in the system and to ensure that it does not lose its initial lustre you must treat it as something that is going to become as firmly established in your organisation's communications network as the telephone or the fax machine.

The first step to guaranteeing that people will use the intranet in the future is to get them hooked at the very beginning. This means that the system has to be simple to use, enjoyable and productive. All of these areas should have been dealt with during the planning and implementation of the system and if it has been done properly then the users will have become fans of the intranet from the outset. In order to keep them on board the intranet has to develop and evolve with the users. Never rest on your laurels and declare that the intranet is finished or that it is working as well as it could be. This is a recipe for disaster – an intranet that stands still is one that withers and dies. Keep seeking feedback and develop the intranet in line with what the users say. The more you do this the more they will feel that the system belongs to them and they will want to see it continuing for the foreseeable future.

After the initial push to win over the customers to the intranet (it is as much a marketing exercise as anything else) the next step to embedding it into your organisation's communications culture is to let the users get on with using it as a work tool. Make sure you are dedicated and conscientious about maintaining and improving the system but scale down the hard sell. You do not have to keep referring to it as revolutionary, innovative, or state-of-the-art. Let the users find this out for themselves and once they have, do not keep reminding them of it. This way the intranet will become accepted as part of everyday working life and, as long as it keeps functioning effectively, the users will not give it a second thought. Nobody now thinks about the impact the telephone has on our lives and if the intranet is accepted in a similar way then we will have undergone a genuine communications revolution.

If the users of an intranet come to view it as just another work tool then the long-term benefits to the organisation will be greatly increased. Productivity will increase as the users become more efficient at using the system and are able to tailor it to their own needs. Also, the more an intranet is used, then the more information will be included on it, thus further reducing costs. The more successful that an intranet is in the short-term, then the more likely it is that it will survive the test of time.

9.7 Summary

- One of the keys to a successful intranet is to keep all of the jargon and computer-speak in the realm of the people who are running and managing the system. Keep the users in blissful ignorance of CGIs, applets, TCP/IP, firewall protocols and Wide Area Networks. Instead, provide them with clear, interesting and informative pages on the intranet.

- Intranets should enable employees to do what is best for the organisation, not necessarily what is best for themselves or the people running the intranet. Empowerment should not be confused with anarchy.

- The intranet is more effective if it is not a stand-alone communications tool. Use it in conjunction with other methods of communication (one-to-one communication, group meetings, notices and e-mail) and make sure that they complement each other and dovetail together. Have a written strategy that shows the role each medium performs.

- The aim of anyone implementing an intranet should be to have it running in the organisation long after they have left. Initially this means winning over the users and then getting people to accept it as a part of everyday life. They will do this if it keeps them supplied with relevant and interesting information and helps them to do their jobs more effectively.

- One of the great pleasures of managing an intranet is seeing the users beginning to create their own pages. Make sure that they are provided with suitable training and guidelines before they try this, or else the result may be frustrating for both parties. Have a definite editorial structure in place so that everyone involved knows what is expected of him or her.

- Make use of the Internet. It can be used as a research tool to find out more about the workings of the intranet or it can be used to promote your organisation. If this is successful in attracting people's attention then the intranet can be used to give them more detailed information.

9.8 Checklist

1 Use the intranet to give the users the information to do their jobs for the ultimate benefit of themselves and the organisation.

2 Do not use the intranet in isolation. It should be used in conjunction with other methods of communication throughout the organisation. This means that the people in control of the intranet should also be aware of the other forms of communication within the organisation.

3 Draw up specific guidelines for users who want to create their own pages. Also invest in some good quality training for them to do this.

4 Be prepared for a more diverse intranet once users are preparing their own pages.

5 Use the Internet to find out the latest news about intranet technology and developments.

6 Draw up an Internet strategy to complement your intranet one.

7 Draw up a long-term strategy for the intranet, illustrating its future role.

10 | USING THE INTRANET AS A BUSINESS TOOL

10.1 Reducing the paper mountain

The concept of the paperless office first crept its way into the mind of the business world with the widespread use of personal computers in the workplace. Since then it has been viewed as anything from an achievable goal to the holy grail of office managers, desperately trying to convince people of its feasibility as they fight their way through a mini-Everest of paper. Most workers would probably associate with the latter of these two views: far from reducing the amount of paper in the workplace, computers, if anything, seem to have had the reverse effect and actually increased the number of items of paper crossing our desks every day.

So why has the promise of a paperless office been turned on its head? The simple answer is the human factor. In theory the use of computers does have the potential to drastically reduce the amount of paper we use. Documents can be created and viewed on screen and e-mail could all but eradicate the need for paper copies of memos and letters. But there are two reasons why the amount of printed paper just keeps growing: it is difficult to read a lot of information on a computer screen; and people do not fully trust computers. The first reason is understandable and depends on how the information is presented. But the second reason comes from the fact that computer users like to print hard copies of documents, 'just in case the computer crashes and deletes the whole lot'. Until this perception is overcome then the paperless office is likely to remain an idealistic utopia.

The use of e-mail is a good example of how technology can increase the amount of paper in circulation. Before the existence of personal computers, if someone wanted to send a memo to a head of department then they wrote to that person and perhaps copied it to a couple of others to whom it was particularly relevant. However, with the use of e-mail the sender can now copy it to dozens of people at the touch of a button, and they do. So instead of three or four people getting the memo, now maybe 15 to 20 receive it. The trouble is when they decide to print it out to keep it, 'for the files', even if it is not directly applicable to them. The result: 20 pieces of paper instead of three. And that is to say nothing of the recipients who then start forwarding the e-mail and sending epistles of their own.

The intranet is one possible solution for the problem of the paperless office. It may not consign the humble piece of paper to the history books but, through its method of presenting information and user-friendly format, it could go a long way to changing the way we use computers.

Getting rid of paper at source

For some items the intranet is already ideal for displaying information on screen without the need to print hard copies. Telephone directories, manuals and handbooks translate easily to the intranet. Large amounts of information can be converted into HTML files and then displayed and accessed on the intranet. This immediately eliminates the need for paper copies of these documents. To make sure that this remains the case the paper copies should be taken away when the intranet version is up and running. This will guarantee that the intranet version is used and it will help to wean people away from the comfort of having a paper copy 'just in case'. As the intranet can be quickly and easily updated it also removes the need to print new copies whenever the information changes. This is particularly true of telephone directories, which are notorious for becoming outdated very quickly and using up enormous amounts of paper in reprints.

Producing documents such as telephone directories, product lists and manuals is an instant 'win-win' situation for the intranet. Not only does it eradicate huge amounts of paper at a stroke, it also gets the users familiar with the idea of viewing information solely on screen. This is the first step to re-educating people about computers and the paper mountain. If they can see that the intranet can be used successfully and efficiently for something that they use everyday, like a telephone directory, then they will have more confidence in it. They will then start considering other ways in which it can be used to limit the number of pieces of paper in circulation. If this way of thinking continues then it will not be too long before the users start making suggestions of their own as to how the intranet can replace paper.

Confidence is a must

The key to this revolution is confidence. The users have to feel that not only is the intranet more efficient at presenting the information but that it will be reliable. This is where the IT aspect becomes a consideration and everything should be done to ensure that the technical side of the system is just as robust as the information that is being put on it.

Presenting the information

The great advantage that the intranet has over e-mail or information in a spreadsheet or a word-processed document is that it can present items in a digestible, easy-to-read format. Instead of having a 10-page document that needs to be scrolled through, the intranet can divide it up into separate files that can be accessed as individual pages as you read through the document. This is vital if you are going to convince the users that the intranet is a feasible candidate for halting the stream of paper around the workplace. Whenever pages are being designed and written in HTML this should be kept at the forefront of the page designer's mind. It is not permissible to merely copy long documents in their entirety and expect the users to patiently scroll their way through them. Through the use of links and separate pages the designer should make it as easy as possible for the user to navigate through the information. People will only favour the intranet over a paper-based system if they feel it is easier to use and presents the information in a visually pleasing format.

If the intranet is to fulfil its potential and become the main source of communication in the workplace then the users have to be won over at the very beginning of the process. It is no use introducing a sub-standard intranet and then, at a later date, replacing it with a new, improved version. By then it will be too late and the users will have returned to the familiarity of their pieces of paper. A great deal of time and attention should be taken to get it right first time and then, if this is done properly, we may see the beginning of the paperless office (or perhaps the term less-paper office is a more realistic one).

10.2 Pooling information

During the average working day most people are usually too busy to consider what benefits there could be from passing on information about their work to other individuals or divisions in the organisation. In the hectic atmosphere of office life it is easy to get so caught up with what you are doing that you do not have the time or inclination to pool resources with others. In many cases this is because it seems to be time-consuming and secondary to the other priorities of working life. However, if ideas, research, training and initiatives are shared then the benefits to the organisation can be dramatic in terms of increased knowledge, awareness and productivity. As a means of communication, the intranet is ideal for achieving this. As a means of encouraging people to share ideas, have a system that rewards innovation – such as an 'idea of the month' scheme.

Sharing research and ideas

In any organisation everyone has his or her own area of interest and expertise. This may be the ability to do shorthand, organise events, find a cure for baldness or split the atom. Whatever it is, there is always a benefit in sharing this information with other employees. The most obvious advantage is that they may discover something that will help them with their own work. This is particularly true if it is an area of common interest. However, employees should not become so blinkered in their work to think that no-one else is interested in what they are doing. The smallest, most seemingly irrelevant piece of information to one person may be the nugget of inspiration that someone else needs to solve a specific problem. And if this information is freely available on the intranet then a multiple sharing of ideas and expertise will be possible – bulletin boards are an excellent method of achieving this.

The second advantage to sharing ideas and initiatives is that it gives everyone a better understanding of what goes on in the organisation. A common complaint in many workplaces is, 'What does Section X actually do?' This can lead to cynicism, resentment and low staff morale, which is a dangerous combination. If everyone can see what everyone else does then people will begin to realise that they are all working together to achieve the same ultimate aims rather than working against each other. An increased understanding of how an entire organisation works gives the employees a greater feeling of belonging, as they can see the bigger picture rather than feeling that they are just chipping away in the dark. In addition, they can offer a better service to external customers because they will feel more confident about answering questions and queries.

The concept of using the intranet to share research ideas and initiatives is particularly useful in the areas of science and education. Much scientific development is based on producing research work and then having other people adding their comments and thoughts. The intranet is the perfect means to enhance and improve this process. Instead of having to produce hard copies of research work and then circulate them to the relevant people, hoping that no-one has been missed out, the scientist can put the information on the intranet and immediately have it available to a much wider audience. This allows for quicker feedback and also, since it can be viewed by a more varied number of people than via a paper-based method, the quality of response may be more diverse. This will result in more debates on the topic and, hopefully, a more rigorous research process.

Information in the classroom

The issue of computers in education is a contentious one, which is hotly debated by all those involved. Supporters claim that they give children much needed IT skills and widen the amount of information that is available to them. The critics argue that computers in schools are generally little more than a distraction that leads to the dumbing-down of education. While these arguments will continue for many years there are two areas where the use of computers can be a benefit to both teachers and pupils. The first is in the user of intranets for individual schools. This is primarily for the benefit of the teachers so they can keep up-to-date with what is going on and share information related to course material and new teaching initiatives. In addition, parts of the intranet can be made available to the pupils to keep them informed about activities such as school trips, open days, sports days and other events happening in the school.

The other area in which computers and intranets can have a major impact on education is distance learning. This is especially useful to schools in remote locations that have a small number of pupils and limited resources as far as teaching staff are concerned. Inevitably in these situations the teacher serves as a 'jack-of-all-trades' since the school may not be able to afford to employ teachers for specialist subjects. In general this works well but it would be unrealistic to expect every teacher to be an expert in the wide range of subjects that fill a school's curriculum. This is where distance learning comes into its own. It can either be in the form of an intranet containing information that the pupils can work through with their own teacher or it can take the form of a video-conference with a teacher who could be hundreds of miles away. This enables specialised teachers, such as art or music teachers, access to pupils who they would otherwise have little chance of seeing. This could be the way ahead for computers in the classroom: providing purpose-built course material that can be targeted at specific age groups. This would seem to be preferable over the increasingly ubiquitous access to the Internet which has led to children spending too much time trying to find information that is relevant to them.

The cost of investing in the necessary equipment for distance learning may initially seem quite high but when this is compared to the cost of employing a full-time teacher then the benefits far outweigh the outlay.

Catching up on conferences and seminars

Another way in which the intranet can be used for pooling information is by enabling people to catch up on seminars, training courses and conferences. This is ideal for employees who have missed courses, or for informing interested parties about what went on at various events. It can also drastically reduce an organisation's training budget because instead of sending five people on a course, one could attend and then produce a summary to put on the intranet. This way, people who did not have the time or opportunity to attend an event will be able to catch up on what was said and any other relevant information.

If the intranet is being used to update employees on conferences or courses then some initial planning needs to be done before the course. If it is a single person attending the event then they should contact the intranet editor beforehand to let them know what the course is about and for any advice on what they might need to bring back from it. The most important item for the intranet is detailed notes of what the course covered. If a group of people are attending the course then one, or preferably two, of them should be nominated to gather the information that is ultimately going to appear on the intranet. The type of information to obtain should include:

- The overall themes of the event
- The speakers and what they said

- New data or ideas that were presented
- Contact groups
- The conclusions or recommendations from the event

At the course the nominated people should not only collect all of the available literature; they should also take their own notes. The reason for this is that copyright considerations will probably restrict you in what you can reproduce from the course literature. If you are producing a summary of the course then it will have to be largely in your own words. Examples from the course can be used but try and avoid quoting verbatim from large chunks of the course literature. If you are in doubt then talk to the course organisers. They may not have any objection to using some of their material but if this is the case they will probably want an acknowledgement included in your summary.

After the course is finished the nominated person can write a summary for the intranet. It should be reasonably brief, while still covering all of the main points. Include a short preface about the person who attended, where they can be contacted and why they attended the event. This is so people who read the summary and are interested in the topic can contact the attendee and obtain more detailed information. In this respect the intranet is acting as a springboard to alert interested parties to the fact that a certain course, seminar or conference has taken place and letting them know where they can find out more. If the intranet is used in this way then no-one should be able to say, 'That course sounded really fascinating, I wish I had gone on it'. Instead of the employee going to the course, the course can come to the employee.

10.3 Linking workers in separate locations

In these days of the global economy an increasing number of organisations have more than one office or headquarters. In some cases this stretches to dozens, or even hundreds, of branch offices. These can be in one country or they could be spread throughout the world. In this instance it is hard to keep all of the employees up-to-date with everything that is happening in the organisation and stop them from feeling that they are cut off from each other. One solution is to use the intranet to unite the separate strands of the company.

Creating a global village

For organisations that are spread over a wide area or in different countries the intranet can be a revelation. Historically it has proved extremely difficult, if not impossible, to keep geographically removed offices, campuses or classrooms up-to-date with the same information at the same time. (Admittedly there are always some items that are relevant to a particular area or location but there is also a large amount of information that is used by every employee.) One of the reasons for this geographical break down in communication is a simple logistical one. If a report is published in London and then has to be mailed, or even faxed, to Los Angeles then it is only natural that the London branch of the organisation will have earlier access to it. With improved communication systems this is becoming less of an issue, but speed of delivery is still important.

The other reason why geographically dispersed organisations sometimes find it hard to circulate the same information at the same time is because it is only human nature to consider your own location before one thousands of miles away. Therefore, a manager in Sydney will be more motivated to impress his own executives rather than those in the organisation's Durban office. This may not necessarily be the best course of action as far as the organisation is concerned but it is only natural to try and impress the people you see everyday, rather than a faceless stranger.

The intranet eliminates any worries about delivery of information or concerns over who sees what and when. As soon as a report, a memo, or a proposal is written it can be posted on the intranet for all to see, whether they are in Vancouver or Venice. As well as creating a more efficient delivery of information this also ensures that all of the company employees, wherever they are, feel as though they are an important part of the overall picture and that they are not being sidelined or forgotten about.

Dealing with a Wide Area Network (WAN)

It would be unrealistic to suggest that an organisation with branches in a dozen countries should transmit exactly the same information to all of them via the intranet. Some items will be applicable to the entire workforce (such as company results, annual reports and restructuring news) while others will only be of local interest. Before the intranet is up and running it will be necessary to consult with a contact point in each of the different locations where the organisation has a base. They will need to know what is going to be on the intranet and then request what general information they want to have access to. This is a delicate balancing act, but remember, each area will probably also be creating intranet pages specifically for themselves.

Once it has been decided what global items are going to be included on the system it is time to start thinking about how these are going to be transmitted around the world. This is where a Wide Area Network (WAN) comes into play. A WAN is the network that links computer systems in separate geographical locations. It could be a single network that operates independently or, as is more likely, it could be created by the amalgamation of two or more Local Area Networks (LANs). For instance, if an organisation has offices in London, Paris and New York then they will each have their own LAN that deals with the information that is relevant to them. However, information that is needed by all of the offices will be placed on the WAN so that it can be accessed by everyone. Figure 10.1 shows the relationship between LANs and WANs.

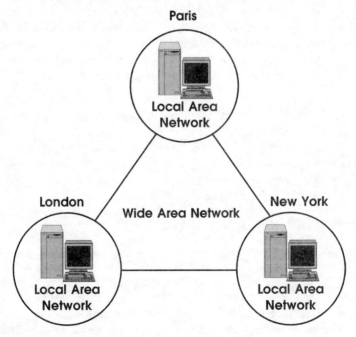

Figure 10.1 How WANs and LANs link together

Maintaining and running a WAN is more time-consuming and intricate than dealing with a localised LAN. The main reason for this is the obvious one: distance. In simple terms it takes longer to transmit data over greater distances and it can be a major headache, making sure that everyone has access to the same information at the same time. With telecommunications technology constantly improving it is certain that the transmission time of data from one server to another will be considerably reduced in the months and years to come.

A more pressing problem for the people running an intranet is to make sure that the data on a WAN is up-to-date and widely accessible. One way of doing this is called 'data replication'. This is where the contents of one server connected to the WAN are sent in their entirety to all of the other servers connected to the system. Since this can put a noticeable strain on the system it is best to think carefully about what information needs to be put on the WAN servers and also how frequently it needs to be updated. For this reason the WAN should only contain the most topical and relevant information from all of the LANs. Ideally it is best to keep one server in each LAN for transmission of information to the WAN. The rest can be used for the transmission and development of local information with the LAN.

Letting people do their own thing

If an intranet stretched across a number of countries then what happens at a local level is almost as important as the shared information that is transmitted along the information superhighway. If each location is given the freedom to express themselves as a separate entity, as well as a sum of the greater part, then this will foster a spirit of independence and self-belief. This is particularly true if the different locations encompass a variety of cultural and religious environments. A similar structure of control for each location is necessary but, within that structure, individuals and divisions should be allowed to produce their own thoughts and ideas. These could subsequently be shared throughout the rest of the organisation, hopefully to the benefit of everyone.

10.4 Summary

- An intranet has the potential to greatly reduce the amount of paper used by an organisation. However, employees feel more secure with hard copies of documents so it may be a long, slow process to wean them away from them. One way to do this is to convince them that the data held on the intranet is not going to disappear off into cyberspace, never to be seen again. A good system of back-ups will reassure them.

- An intranet is ideal for sharing ideas, information and research. This is particularly applicable in the areas of science and education and its role as a teaching tool should not be underestimated.

- Wide Area Networks (WANs) can be used to link workers in separate geographical locations. Careful consideration should be given to the information that is included for general distribution and what is kept at each local level.

10.5 Checklist

1 Draw up a realistic plan for reducing paper usage by putting documents on the intranet. Include a method for persuading users not to make hard copies of everything on the system.

2 List all of the items that could be put solely on the intranet, such as telephone directories. If this is done, you must ensure that people travelling away from the office have access to the Internet, generally via a laptop computer.

3 Ask different departments to submit intranet material about what they do. Suggest that they do this as if they are explaining it to someone who has no idea about their work.

4 Ask for list of training courses, seminars and conferences that people are attending. Then contact them and ask them if they would like to summarise it for the intranet.

5 Keep all users in mind when you are dealing with an intranet, even if they are on a separate continent.

6 Sub-divide the intranet into different sections for employees in different geographical locations.

11 | MEASURING THE BENEFITS

11.1 Surveying via the intranet

After an intranet has been up and running for six months to a year, you may need to produce some hard evidence to show that it is a success and that it is achieving its goals of saving money and producing a better informed workforce. The first of these can be done by before-and-after cost analysis (see below) while the second can be achieved by direct contact with the people who are using the intranet. It is all very well having a folder full of anecdotal evidence suggesting that employees think the intranet is the best thing since the office tea break. But if you do not have hard facts to back this up then senior management may pour scorn on the performance of the system.

There are a number of ways you can elicit the views of intranet users:

- By telephone
- By letter
- By the intranet itself

While telephone and letter are viable options they are not perfect. A telephone survey could catch the users cold, leading to less well thought-out responses, while paper correspondence can be slow and time-consuming. The ideal method is the intranet itself. Since you are promoting the benefits of the system it makes sense to use it for surveying the users. This will demonstrate that not only is the intranet a tool for displaying information, but also that it is suitable for two-way communications.

Methods of surveying

It is virtually impossible to go through life without becoming well acquainted with surveys, market research, opinion polls or questionnaires. They appear from all angles, quizzing us on anything from our favourite washing powder, to how often we go on holiday. Invariably such surveys or questionnaires are brushed aside or filed directly into the bin. The cause for this is not just because we balk at the thought of another double-glazing offer, but more often than not because the questionnaire or survey is too long and daunting. When faced with something that stretches to several pages the immediate reaction of most people is, 'Sorry, I don't have time'.

When conducting a survey on the intranet it is important to keep the length, number and complexity of questions to a minimum. It is better to get answers to half a dozen questions than to get no response from 50 questions. The first area to deal with is the format of the survey. Ideally, it should consist of a small number of well thought-out questions that only require a Yes or No answer, or an Agree, Disagree response. If you ask open-ended questions, hoping that the users will write an extensive dialogue in reply, then you may be disappointed. People sometimes feel uneasy or tongue-tied about writing their own reply so it is better to ask for a specific response and then have the option of including general comments at the end of the questionnaire. The questions that are asked should be positive and upbeat, with an aim of gaining similar responses. However, do not put words into the mouths of the respondents by asking leading questions. The types of questions could include:

- Do you feel your productivity has improved since using the intranet?
- Do you have a better understanding of what is going on in the organisation?
- Do you believe the information you receive on the intranet is accurate and up-to-date?
- Do you believe that you receive information more quickly than before?
- Does the intranet help you do your job more effectively?
- Would you miss the intranet if it were removed?

The physical methods of surveying via the intranet are twofold. You can either create a questionnaire that can be printed from the screen and then sent to a central point. However, this creates unnecessary paper usage and a better method is to have the survey filled in on screen and then returned via the computer network. This can be achieved through the use of HTML forms, which enables two-way electronic communication via the intranet.

Analysing results

When the responses to a survey start coming in, it is important to keep an open mind and not have preconceived notions about what they will say. You might have your own ideas about the intranet but the whole purpose of the exercise is to find out what the users think. Once the users have spoken you will have to take some form of action based on what they have said (unless of course the responses are overwhelmingly positive). If you do not act then the users will think that you do not take their views seriously and so your own credibility, and that of the intranet, will be undermined.

The first thing to do following a survey is to contact the users and thank them for their participation. If the views are generally favourable then you can compile a report based on this and pass it to senior management. This will demonstrate that the users of the intranet view it as a success and it serves its purpose of enabling them to do their jobs more effectively.

Making improvements

If a survey throws up suggested improvements to the system then the first thing to do is to remedy any perceived faults. Again, you may not agree with it, but if the general consensus of the users is that something is a problem then it has to be sorted out. This may cover content, presentation or delivery of information, and the comments of the users should be taken very seriously. If they do not like the system then they will not use it. Once the problem areas have been overcome, you can re-survey the users and, if the response is favourable, send your report to senior management.

Although surveys via the intranet are an excellent way of finding out what the users think of the system and how they would improve it, it is best to use them sparingly. One every six months would be more than enough — any more and the users may start to suffer from survey burnout. As long as intranet surveys are concise and enable the system to evolve positively, the users will soon come to accept them as an integral part of the process.

11.2 Analysing cost benefits

One of the great claims made for intranets is that they can save organisations significant amounts of money. While this is undoubtedly true, hard-nosed accountants will want to see documentary evidence to support this. State of the art technology cuts little ice with the moneymen if it does not show a surplus in the profit column. Throughout the planning, implementation and management of an intranet, the concept of cost savings from the system should be kept firmly on the agenda.

It is never too early to start calculating how the intranet is going to save your organisation money. In fact, this should be addressed even before it is up and running. The most obvious way that an intranet can cut costs is in reducing the amount of paper used in an organisation and so reducing costs for buying, printing and distributing the paper itself. When you are planning what to put onto the system, you should work out how much paper is currently used and how much you think this will be reduced with the use of the intranet. The most common areas of high paper usage are:

- Telephone directories (particularly if updated regularly)
- Daily or weekly notices that are distributed to all staff
- Work practice manuals
- Newsletters and magazines
- Product information updates

Calculating the savings

To analyse how much paper the intranet could save, you should initially calculate the volume of paper that is generated before the system is in place. For a general figure you could check with your printing or reprographic department to see how much paper they order in six months or a year and use this as a rough calculation. However, since this may include a variety of miscellaneous items, it is much better to do an actual calculation based on the above items and the number of people in your organisation. This way you will have a working number of how much paper is used before the introduction of the intranet. It should also be possible to allocate a precise figure per person for the amount of paper they receive in any given time period (this should be at least quarterly to includ as many different types of correspondence as possible).

The next part of the calculation involves looking at your implementation programme to see who is getting the intranet and when. From this you will be able to work out the reduction in the amount of paper used over a particular period of time. For example, if your organisation has 1,000 employees and they each receive 500 sheets of paper a year (or approximately

40 sheets per month), then this is an annual total of 500,000. If your implementation programme allows for 50 users to be connected to the intranet every month, this equates to 2,000 fewer sheets of paper being used each month. Over the course of a year this will translate into 600 users being connected to the intranet and 300,000 fewer sheets of paper being used. This is a considerable saving because as well as the cost of buying, printing and distributing the paper there is also the issue of storage. If your organisation is using 300,000 fewer sheets of paper every year, this means that the space this would have taken up in storage is now free to be used for something else.

Although the intranet can generate large savings in relation to paper costs there a couple of points to bear in mind when you are calculating the potential savings:

1 The amount of paper that the intranet saves may not be an absolute figure, as users may print off hard copies of items on the intranet. This could happen for a variety of reasons, the main one being that, initially, users might feel more comfortable with the back-up of a paper copy as well as the electronic version. In time, you should be able to persuade them away from this safety-net mentality.

2 The paper savings need to be offset against the cost of creating and maintaining the intranet. This involves the human resources used and the overall cost of running the intranet. How this is calculated will vary from organisation to organisation and it may well be something that is dealt with by the finance department. Whatever the costs involved, they are likely to be considerably less then the savings that the system can generate.

11.3 Analysing time savings

Intranets can not only generate measurable savings in the form of reduced paper and printing costs, they can also save organisations money by giving employees the means to do their jobs more quickly and efficiently. These can be harder to quantify than the more obvious cost savings but they can include some of the following:

- Spending less time finding correct telephone extensions throughout the organisation since the most up-to-date numbers are on the intranet. This not only saves time for employees but also gives a better service for external customers trying to contact specific people.

- Personal details can be updated quickly and easily on screen, without the need for the time-consuming process of numerous paper forms passing back and forth.

- Items of news and information can be available on the intranet more quickly than if they had to be printed and distributed, giving employees more time to act or react.

- Product information can be updated quickly, thus saving time for the sales force.

Although it is fairly easy to calculate tangible savings made from using less paper, it is not quite so simple to say what type of savings are made through improved productivity and awareness. This is one area where it really is preferable to turn to management consultants to assess the efficiency savings made through the intranet. They are experienced in undertaking this type of study and they should be able to provide you with a professional and comprehensive report covering what improvements the intranet has brought to your organisation. When you are looking for consultants for this purpose it is best to employ a company which has experience of assessing intranets, so that they have a good idea of what they are dealing with from the outset. Due to the increasing number of management consultants with IT experience it should be no problem finding someone who is well versed in the intricacies of the intranet.

11.4 Dealing with an informed workforce

Any organisation that can confidently say that it has a well-informed workforce is either very lucky or else very well run. Since luck rarely plays a part in matters such as these, it would almost certainly be the latter. Educating people about what goes on within an organisation is no easy matter; but the benefits to be gained are substantial. Certain measures have to be taken in order to establish a well-informed workforce:

- Employees need to be provided with relevant information.
- The information must be kept updated and current.
- The process of getting the information to the employees must

make them feel valued. (It is no good just barking instructions at people and expecting them to be grateful for it.)

- Employees should feel that they are in an 'information circle', i.e. they can pass on their own views and ideas as well as receiving them from others.

- There should be checks in place to make sure that employees are getting the right information.

The intranet fulfils all of these criteria, as it is the ideal tool for giving and receiving information. In addition it is enjoyable to use (or should be if it has been designed properly) and allows the users to feel that they are a valid part of the communications process, not just sitting on the sidelines waiting to be told something. This not only generates an informed workforce but also a contented one – everyone likes to feel included and if they do they are happier, which can only be good for the individual and the organisation.

The benefits from an informed workforce are not only seen within an organisation. They can also have a dramatic effect on external clients and customer relations. Even a simple task like answering the telephone and being able to find the correct extension number first time can have a significant impact on the way an organisation is viewed. Get it right and the customer remembers an efficient and professional service. Get it wrong and an image of inefficiency and bungling remains. With a current internal telephone directory on the intranet, employees will be able to get it right every time.

The impact of an efficient and knowledgeable workforce cannot be over-estimated. Customer relations are now recognised as performing a vital role in the business equation and large sums of money are being invested in improving performance in this area. If the intranet can play a part in achieving this, then it should be seen as an essential investment.

11.5 Looking at customer reaction

If an intranet is effective and successful then it will not only benefit the workforce in making their jobs more enjoyable and productive but it will also ultimately benefit customers and clients. Since pleasing the customers is the core aim of most organisations, it is important to look at some of the benefits that can be passed onto customers both directly and indirectly via the intranet.

The most direct benefit that customers and clients can gain from an intranet is an additional source of information through the creation of an extranet. This is when certain parts of an intranet are made available to a selected external audience. This allows the customers to have instant access to information such as:

- Latest products and new developments
- Pricing changes
- Annual reports and accounts
- Expansion news

This is information that customers could obtain by other methods but an extranet allows them to get immediate access to it without having to approach the organisation and ask for it. In addition, if the intranet is being run and managed efficiently, the information on the extranet will be the latest available, so the customer will be able to plan accordingly, armed with up-to-date data.

As well as the direct benefit of obtaining relevant and current information, customers will also benefit from an effective intranet in their dealing with the employees. If the organisation's intranet is doing its job then the workforce will be better informed and more motivated. This in turn will translate into an improved customer service in terms of information being readily available and staff being more willing to help.

Surveying customers

Finding out what customers think of the intranet may be slightly problematic because they might not even be aware of the fact that your organisation has one. If your customer service has improved dramatically the very fact of the matter will be enough for your clients; they will not be overly concerned about how you have achieved it. So in order to gauge customer reaction you may have to tell them what you have done and then ask them if this has led to a significant improvement in the way they are treated. This can be done in a number of formats:

- A mailshot, to either a selected number, or all, of the organisations on your mailing list.

- A telephone survey, conducted either internally or by consultants.

- Through the extranet, using the same type of system as you would for an internal survey on the intranet.

Begin your survey by saying that you are/have updating/updated your internal communications system and that you hope it will bring benefits, both internally and externally. Then ask them to answer three or four questions, preferably in a YES/NO format, and ask them if they have any general comments. The types of question that you should ask include:

- Have you noticed an improvement in the speed of response to enquiries?

- Has information provided been more detailed and reliable?

- Do the employees seem better informed about the service they are providing?

- Are you confident of receiving an efficient service when you contact our organisation?

As with any survey you must be prepared to act on the results. If it highlights a perceived problem for clients, action must be taken. Even if the intranet is considered a success by staff, it should still be looked at to see whether this is the cause of the problem. However, the fault may lie with another part of the organisation's communications strategy, so all aspects of the system must be examined. The chances are that if an intranet is considered to be a success internally, it will translate externally to customers.

11.6 Summary

- Once your intranet has been up and running for a reasonable length of time, you should ask the users what they think of the system. Be prepared for a range of comments. Where necessary, act upon the suggestions, since it is the users who will ultimately judge whether the intranet is a success or not.

- Working out how much money an intranet is saving is a vital part of the overall, long-term strategy. Prepare a model for the way your organisation distributed information before and after the intranet was in place. There should also be accurate calculations for tangible cost savings.

- Savings from an intranet are also made in terms of improved efficiency and time saved. These can be difficult to quantify so it is a good idea to employ a firm of management consultants to do this.

- If an intranet is working well then external customers should see advantages in the form of a more reliable and effective customer service.

- If you want to find out what your customers think about your intranet and the effect it has, then you must listen to what they have to say, even if it means changing something on the intranet. It is no use thinking you have the best intranet in the world if it leads to you losing customers and business.

11.7 Checklist

1 Design a survey to send to users of the intranet.

2 Keep your survey short and rely on YES/NO answers.

3 List all of the items that have been transferred from paper copies onto the intranet. Use this to calculate the savings that have been made.

4 Make sure that the intranet gives employees the information that they want.

5 Get quotes from a number of consultants to measure improved efficiency among staff.

6 Devise a strategy for surveying customers in relation to improvements that have come about from the intranet.

12 | LOOKING TO THE FUTURE

12.1 Predicting growth

With the dramatic developments in information technology in the 1990s it is almost certain that the rise of intranet use will continue unabated into the 21st century. The provision of information is very much a growth industry: the Internet, intranets, digital broadcasting and improved telecommunications facilities are shaping a global society that is hungry for more and more information. In the workplace the intranet, or at least a descendant of it, will help feed this voracious appetite.

Assessing how quickly intranets will develop will never be an exact science, but most of the predictions point to a considerable growth on a world-wide basis. There have been numerous surveys making various claims about intranets. These should always be viewed carefully since predictions have been known not to transpire. Some of the claims include:

- By 1999 the world-wide Internet market will be worth $43 billion. Intranets will account for more than half of this.
- By 2000 there will be over 4 million intranet servers compared with 440,000 for the Internet.
- The estimated number of intranet users by the year 2001 will be 133 million.
- By 2001 intranets will account for more than 20% of all IT spending.

There are several organisations that specialise on providing, among other things, data on intranet and Internet growth and development. Three of them who have sites on the Internet are:

International Data Corporation   http://www.idc.com/
Forrester   http://www.forrester.com/
NUA Internet Surveys   http://www.nua.ie/surveys/

It is a good idea to check these sites at regular intervals because IT surveying is almost as much of a growth industry as the systems themselves. New surveys are produced and posted on the Internet on an almost daily basis.

12.2 Assessing longevity

As with any relatively new technological development it is hard to predict how the product will stand the test of time – at the time of its release the Betamax video recorder was thought to be a worldbeater but this proved to be misguided. At first glance, the future of the intranet seems linked inextricably to the development of the Internet since it uses the same technology. However, this is only part of the story: the real growth and development will depend largely on the use of personal computers (PCs) and, equally importantly, computer networks, in the workplace.

Without computers joined by a network, intranets would not exist. However, with computers being increasingly used in the workplace throughout the world (this obviously varies from country to country) our dependency on them is going to get greater, not less. And with the use of computers, comes the creation of networks – computers that are connected together so that they can communicate between each other rather than exist as stand-alone machines. It is these networks (either Local Area Networks or Wide Area Networks) that are essential to the future development of the intranet.

So far the signs for future development are promising. In the United States (which is always the most accurate barometer for the use of new technologies) the analysts and forecasters, Forrester, recently reported that over 60% of the companies that they contacted who did not have intranets at present were planning to invest in one in the near future. In the UK, a Prodata survey found that 97% of companies with more than 50 employees were using PCs, and 50% of all employees were using PCs. Perhaps more significantly, over 65% of PCs were connected to a Local Area Network. If this pattern of growth in networks continues then a comparable increase in the use of intranets is inevitable.

12.3 Developing intranets and the Internet

So while the future of the intranet in relation to computer networks seems secure, what of its relationship and development with the Internet? Of the two, the intranet has a more clearly established identity, being a tool for communicating business information. But the Internet is a sprawling mass of information that serves different purposes for different groups of people. There is a huge potential for intranets to be greatly enhanced by integrating further into the Internet but for this to happen the latter will have to change.

At present the Internet is perfectly acceptable for the recreational user who has time to explore the numerous tangents that occur on the World Wide Web. Indeed, to the early converts to the Internet, or 'netheads' as they are sometimes disparagingly referred to, the system has already become too mainstream.

Business users do not have the luxury of time on their hands. They want business information and they want it quickly. To them, large tracts of the Internet are of no use and merely serve to slow down the system. And as the consumer-led demand for more information expands, so businesses and organisation will be forced to seek quicker access to the Internet. They will also want to be able to log-on to a system that only holds the type of information that they and their clients require. So this suggests there is a demand for a business orientated Internet and also one that is available for the computer enthusiasts and programmers.

A third factor can also be added to this equation — the recreational users who want to use the Internet, or at least the technology, to capitalise on the growth in digital broadcasting. These are people who have no interest in surfing the Internet, or even sending e-mails. However, they want the freedom to choose what television programmes and videos they watch, and when they watch them. This technology is already with us, using fibre-optic cables and domestic electricity supplies to deliver huge volumes of digital information. And if the software companies get their way, as they inevitably seem to do, this information will be controlled by something very similar to the present day web browsers. In addition to customised home entertainment systems, people will also be able to conduct tasks such as banking and shopping by using a browser and their television set. This may not do much for our levels of health or fitness, but it will certainly revolutionise the way we live our lives.

Re-inventing the Internet

So, if the Internet evolves in this three-tier way it may cease to exist in its current form. The largest part will probably be the entertainment sector, which will be like a glorified way of watching television; the technical, boffin-based part of the Internet will pass back into the hands of the people who invented the system; and the rest will belong to the business world. Ideally, this will become genuine business information, with all of the cyberspace junk that currently inhabits the Internet stripped away. This may even lead to certain levels of regulation, at least in terms of what is put on the system. This is already happening and the global business community is currently trying to formulate framework regulations to control the world-wide use of electronic commerce (e-commerce).

If the commercial world does eventually get its own business-based Internet then this can only be good news for the intranet. If businesses and organisations know the Internet will deliver specific business benefits then they are more likely to get connected and do so through an intranet. Then, as more organisations go online, the customer demand for information will lead to a greater sharing of corporate details, leading to sections of company intranets being made available to the wider business community (extranets). If this is done in a focused, professional manner then eventually the boundaries between the Internet, intranets and extranets will become blurred to the point where they are operating as one large pool of information. Of course there will always be a need for organisations to keep parts of their intranets for internal eyes only, but if the business world can succeed in obtaining its own niche in the Internet then the future of the intranet is not only secure, it is likely to blossom.

12.4 Using new technology

The future is here

Just as the first telephone bears little resemblance to the palm-sized contraptions that are used today, so it is likely that the intranets of the 21st century will be significantly different from the versions that are currently in use. In some cases, the future is already upon us. For anyone who is seriously committed to the intranet as the way forward for corporate communication, the idea of holding meetings on the intranet via video-conferencing is an attractive one. Although this may seem like science fiction to some people it is already with us and in use.

This increasingly popular device enables employees to communicate face-to-face without having to leave their desks. It is also an ideal method for linking people in different geographical locations. The advantages to a large organisation are considerable:

- People save both time and money in not having to physically travel to the location of a meeting. This may just be to another floor in the office or it could be hundreds of miles away.
- Meetings are scheduled more easily because the participants can remove the travelling time from their timetables.
- Several shorter, informal meetings can replace the longer more formal varieties.

However, there is a downside to video conferencing:

- There is no actual human contact, just virtual interaction. There will be times when it is beneficial for people to meet person-to-person rather than via a computer screen. A sensible balance between the two needs to be achieved for it to be fully effective.

Although video conferencing technology is still in its infancy as far as its development is concerned it is surprisingly inexpensive to install. Video-conferencing cameras are relatively cheap as is the software used to run it (and in some cases it is free).

Other developments

Due to the speed at which computing technology develops, predicting what will happen in years to come is a bit like trying to guess the winners of the Oscars in five years' time. But some of the most likely developments are:

- Increased power and speed. This almost goes without saying in an industry where computers are outdated even before they have left the manufacturer's warehouse. Speed of delivery of information on intranets and the amount of data that can comfortably be stored on them will almost certainly double, at least, within the next two or three years.
- Increasingly user-friendly desktop computers. This will probably involve a greater use of touch-screen terminals and also voice-activated software.
- More interactive functions for the users.
- Improved security in the form of encrypted code words and smartcards, to allay fears about people gaining unlawful

access to an intranet. This is currently one of the major concerns
for organisations considering developing an intranet.

Some of these are already with us, and the best way to keep up-to-date
with the latest technological developments is to scan the Web sites of the
manufacturers of computer hardware and software. The Further
Information section at the end of the book lists various useful Web sites.

12.5 Discovering initiatives

At the time of writing, a search of 'intranets' on one of the popular search
engines on the Internet produced over 600,540 suggested sites. Of these,
tens of thousands of them are little more than company advertising,
outdated information or small items of little or no relevance. However, in
amongst the vast wealth of electronic data there are nuggets of information
that can be used to improve and advance your intranet. These can
sometimes be found by refining your search criteria. For instance, if you
want to find out the latest developments in Java programming then a
search involving the words 'intranet' and 'Java' will produce thousands
of suggested sites.

In addition to a general search of the Internet to find out the latest
developments in the world of intranets you could try specific contact with
people who are involved with them. Again, this can be done via the Internet
and there are two ways to approach it.

Write to the author

The first method is to find articles about the relevant intranet topic that
you are interested in and then e-mail the author asking them for further
details or advice. This is a relatively simple operation because authors
frequently include their e-mail addresses at the end of articles. This is a
good way to interact with the people who are involved in the development
of intranets and they will probably be able to give you some useful contacts.
One factor to bear in mind when you are doing this is that even though e-
mail is a very fast way of communicating with people, they may not answer
you query or request immediately. This is because once an e-mail address
is on the Internet it is inevitable that the person involved will receive
dozens, if not hundreds, of communications and so it will take them some
time to answer them all.

Use the newsgroups

The second way to contact people who are interested in intranets is to join an Internet newsgroup and ask for information there. Newsgroups are a part of the Internet, which operate like a club where all of the members can air their views and ideas. If you have a connection to the Internet then you will be able to join and participate in a newsgroup. This is a slightly more hit or miss method of looking for information because there is no way of knowing what the other members of the newsgroup will be interested in. However, with an Internet related topic such as intranets there will undoubtedly be a large number of people who will want to offer advice and comments.

Teach Yourself the Internet

The focus of this book is intranets, not the Internet. To find out more about the World Wide Web, newsgroups and other aspects of the Internet, you might like to try *Teach Yourself the Internet* by Mac Bride.

12.6 Looking at global implications

Given the rapid development and expansion of the Internet and intranets in the 1990s it is fair to assume that this will continue for the foreseeable future. If this happens then there are some important implications for the global business community, particularly if the Internet and intranets begin to merge into more of a single entity.

The first priority for the business world is to ensure that the future development of the Internet and intranets is undertaken in a way that is conducive to their needs and aspirations. As discussed above, this may mean separating the elements of the Internet so that there is a system that is dedicated solely to the needs of the business community. If this happens then there will need to be detailed and widespread debate about the best way to use the new communications technology.

The big worry is that the major players who control the computer software and hardware will be in a dangerously strong position to dictate the future of a business-based Internet and so have a considerable advantage over many areas of the business world. To avoid this there will need to be determined and dedicated action in the business world to prevent the creation of communications 'super-powers'. This is already happening to a certain extent, with particular concern being expressed at the role of some of the software multinational giants. As with many aspects of the business world it will undoubtedly come down to survival of the fittest and those who do not keep up with the technological developments will find the going difficult.

The second factor that will have an important impact on the role of intranets and the Internet in the global business community is the development and spread of telecommunications technology around the world. While telephone usage per capita is high in areas such as the North America, Europe and Australasia it is a different picture in many other parts of the world such as Africa and Asia. In China for instance, a population of 1 billion is served by only approximately 10 million telephone connections. In recent years several major telecommunications companies have tried to expand into China but they have found progress slow due to the amount of red tape they have to deal with. However it seems only a matter of time before the boundaries of world markets are extended further and further. Once the technology is in place in all parts of the world we will then see a true global economy based on sophisticated communications technology. Intranets and the Internet will be at the heart of this revolution as they link businesses, clients and customers from Alaska to Zimbabwe.

The third implication for the world of commerce is how the spread of the intranet will effect the geographical appearance of the business community. As the power and influence of intranets spreads it is likely that this will have a dramatic impact on how businesses manage their real estate needs and where they locate their workforce. For large areas of the business community such as financial services, computing, legal services and telecommunications the physical location of their offices will become unimportant as far as the customers are concerned, since all transactions could be done via computers. Therefore businesses will relocate to cheaper locations and the commercial districts that are presently in large cities will cease to exist in their present form. A much smaller presence may still be maintained but the bulk of the workforce will be located elsewhere.

To take this one step further, the number of employees working from home could increase dramatically as the power and influence of the intranet spreads. If someone can get all of the internal information that they need from their intranet, and switch to the Internet for any external items they require, or to e-mail clients or customers, then there will be no need for them to move from a computer in their own home. And with the expansion of video-conferencing they will even be able to take part in meetings and discussions with colleagues. There are various social implications that are attached to an expansion in home working, such as time-management and interaction with colleagues. Therefore it seems likely that this is an area that many companies will have to investigate in the near future.

12.7 Summary

- All of the available data suggests a strong growth in the use of intranets by the new millennium and beyond.
- For the intranet to become a long-lasting part of the business world the development of intranets and the Internet has to be looked at in unity.
- Intranet technology is changing and improving on an almost daily basis. The Internet is the best way to keep up with the latest developments. Searches under specific topics can be undertaken or direct e-mails sent to people who have written about intranets on the Internet. There are also newsgroups that can offer a forum for intranet discussions.
- As telecommunications technology around the world improves, so will the importance of the intranet.
- If intranets and the Internet continue to grow at their current rate, then the way business is conducted around the world could change significantly. More and more organisations will feel the need to join the communications revolution and regulations may need to be introduced to ensure that control does not fall into the hands of the few. In addition, the geographical face of the business world may change as organisations relocate and more employees work from their computers at home.

GLOSSARY

ActiveX: A Microsoft programming language that allows for interactive elements to be included on an intranet (see also Java).

Applets: A mini program that can be embedded in an HTML page, written in the Java language (see Java).

Browser: The piece of software which allows users to view HTML pages, on an intranet or the World Wide Web, in an accessible and user-friendly fashion. The two most popular ones are Netscape Navigator and Microsoft Internet Explorer.

Common Gateway Interface (CGI) script: A device that enables intranet users to access information that is held outside the intranet itself.

Cyberspace: The abstract world inhabited by computer networks and their users.

E-mail: The method of sending electronic messages via the Internet or an intranet.

Extranet: Parts of an intranet that are made available to a wider, external, audience.

Firewall: A piece of software that acts as a security barrier between an intranet and an external source.

Graphical Interchange Format (GIF): A file format for graphics. Particularly useful for icon and animations.

Hacker: A person who tries to gain unauthorised access to a computer system.

Home Page: The first page of an intranet or web site, generally containing a contents list or map to the rest of the system.

HyperText Markup Language (HTML): A computer formatting code that is used to create documents that can then be read and displayed by a browser.

Information Superhighway: A term used to describe the means by which electronic data is communicated among computers and computer networks.

Internet: The system that connects millions of computer and their users around the world.

Internet Explorer: Microsoft's browser (see *Browser*).

Internet Service Provider (ISP): Companies who provide access to the Internet. There is usually a charge for this, but some companies offer a free service.

Intranet: An internal version of the Internet that can be used as a powerful internal communications tool for organisations and companies.

Java: A programming language that can create software that is platform-independent. This means that they can operate on a variety of computers and computer systems.

Joint Photographic Experts Group (JPEG): A file format for graphics. Particularly useful for photographs as JPEG files take up relatively little disk space.

Link: An HTML device that acts as a shortcut between pages. By clicking on a link the user is taken straight to the linked page.

Local Area Network (LAN): A group of computers in close proximity that are linked together so that they can share the same information.

Macintosh OS: The network operating system for Apple Macintosh computers.

Modem: The device that links a computer to the Internet, via a telephone socket. A modem is not required with an intranet.

Navigator: Netscape's browser (see *Browser*).

Network: A group of computers linked to share the same data and other resources.

Network Operating System (NOS): The software that enables a group of networked computers to function. These include Novell Netware and Window NT.

Operating System (OS): The software that enables individual computers to function — the brains of the system.

Personal Computers (PCs): Computers that are based on the IBM design and which are invariably run by a Microsoft Operation System. By far the most common type of computer in use today.

Random Access Memory (RAM): The memory storage space on a computer that is used to undertake operation while the system is in use. The larger the amount of RAM then the quicker the computer can perform tasks and requests.

Read Only Memory (ROM): Memory storage space that holds data that is permanent and cannot usually be altered.

Search Engine: A device for finding specific information on an intranet or the Internet. In most cases the user types in the topic that they want to see and then the Search Engine goes and looks for it on the system.

Servers: The heart of an intranet. This is where the intranet files are stored and the users access them by requesting the information via their browser. The server then sends out the relevant files.

Transmission Control Protocol/Internet Protocol (TCP/IP): The electronic means by which computers in a network are connected together and are able to communicate with each other.

UNIX: A multi-tasking, multi-user operating system, renowned for its robust performance.

Virus: A program that can enter a computer or a computer network and damage the data that is held there. Viruses can either just constitute nuisance value or they can be of a destructive nature.

Web Authoring: The process of creating pages for an intranet or the Internet. Pages can either be created with an HTML editor or Web Authoring software package (see WYSIWYG).

Wide Area Network (WAN): Similar to a LAN except that it connects computers over a much wider geographical area.

Windows: The Microsoft operating system that is used in most PCs.

World Wide Web (WWW): The pages of information that are accessed through the Internet. There are literally millions of pages on the Web, produced by a range of people, from individuals to multinational companies.

WYSIWYG: The acronym for 'What You See Is What You Get'. This is used in word-processing, desktop publishing and page design to describe software where the screen display is exactly as it will appear in the final output or when viewed through a browser.

FURTHER INFORMATION

Useful Internet Addresses

Animations

http://www.mindworkshop.com/alchemy/gcsdemo.html
http://www.microsoft.com/imagecomposer
http://www.gifanimations.com/animated.shtml
http://www.tiac.net/users/gstudio/an1.html
http://www.wanders2.co/rose/animate3.html

Backgrounds, colours and images

http://www.infi.net/wwwimages/colorindex.html
http://www.ine.com/Web/Examples/rgb.html
http://www.pixelfoundry.com//bgs.html
http://textures.guinet.com/index.html
http://www.vision-web.net/graphics/
http://www.ip.pt/webground/
http://www.village.vossnet.co.uk/h/henrys/bkex.htm
http://busines.auracom.com/wurld/kitrex3.html

Browsers

Explorer http://www.microsoft.com/
Navigator http://www.netscape.com/

Computer software and hardware companies

Microsoft http://www.microsoft.com/
Novell http://www.novell.com/
IBM http://www.ibm.com/
Hewlett Packard http://www.hewlett-packard.com/
Sun Microsystems http://www.sun.com/
Apple http://www.apple.com/

Frames

http://www.davesite.com/webstation/html/chap14.shtml

HTML Editors

http://www.webweaver.com/
http://www.faico.net/dida/

HTML Resource

http://www.quest.internet.co.uk/drh/HTML/index.html
http://www.ncsa.uiuc.edu/General/
http://members.aol.com/Rick1515/index.htm
http://www.pageresource.com/
http://www.microsoft.com/msdownload/#pubtool

Java and ActiveX

http://www.javasoft.com/doc
http://www.gamelan.com/
http://www.microsoft.com/activex/

Research Organisations

International Data Corporation http://www.idc.com/
Forrester http://www.forrester.com/
NUA Internet Surveys http://www.nua.ie/surveys/

Search Tools

Yahoo http://www.yahoo.com/
AltaVista http://www.altavista.digital.com/
Excite http://www.excite.com/
Verity SEARCH '97 http://www.verity.com/
CompassWare InfoMagnet http://www.compassware.com/
Adobe Acrobat Search http://www.adobe.com/
Quarterdeck WebCompass http://www.quarterdeck.com/

Tables

http://home.tampabay.rr.com/webhelp/tables/
http://members.aol.com/harvillo/tabtut.html

Web page authoring

Microsoft FrontPage http://www.microsoft.com/frontpage/
Adobe PageMill http://www.adobe.com/prodindex/
pagemill/main.html
NetObjects Fusion http://www.netobjects.com/

*Note: When entering an Internet address you do not have to include the
initial 'http://' as this will be done automatically by the system.*

Further reading

Bookshop shelves are groaning under the weight of publications on computer-related topics and a fair number of these relate to intranets and the Internet. These cover a wide variety of subjects and also cater to different levels of users. The following is just a very small selection of what is on offer and a good idea is to drop into your local bookshop or library and see what they have available.

- *Teach Yourself HTML: Publishing on the World Wide Web*, Mac Bride, Hodder & Stoughton
- *Teach Yourself The Internet*, Mac Bride, Hodder & Stoughton
- *Teach Yourself Java*, Wright, Hodder & Stoughton
- *The ABC of Intranets*, Dyson, Coleman and Gilbert, Sybex
- *Networking Essential Unleashed*, Sportack, SAMS Publishing
- *Dan Gookin's Web Wambooli*, Gookin, Peachpit Press
- *Internet Complete*, various, Sybex
- *Computer User's Dictionary*, Microsoft Press
- *Firewalls Complete*, Goncalves, McGraw-Hill

INDEX

H

Hackers 109
Heading tags 37
Home Page 30, 69, 70
Home working 156
Horizontal rules 36
htm extension 35
HTML authoring 33
HTML editor 34
Human Resource divisions 18
HyperText Markup Language 28

I

Image source tag 45
Images 43
Implementation, consistency 88
Indexing 103
Information sharing 131
Information overload 112
Information technology 1
Interactive intranet 17
Interactivity 8
Internal communications strategy
      118
Internet
   harnessing 121
   marketing on 123
Internet link 22
Internet site 123
Intranet
   defined 1
   demonstration 13
   interactive 17
   read-only 16
   structure 73
IT supplements 15
Italics 36

J

Jargon 115
Java 49
JavaScript 49

Joint Photographic Experts Group
      (JPEG or JPG) 43

K

Keywords 103

L

Levi-Strauss 17
Limiting access 22
Line breaks 36
Linking locations 134
Links in HTML 41
LINUX 85
Local Area Networks (LANs) 4,
      136
Long-term targets 25
Longevity 150

M

Macintosh OS 85
Marquees 61
Microsoft FrontPage Editor 63

N

NetObjects Fusion 64
Netscape 28
Netscape Navigator 29
Network Operating System 85
Networks 85
News section 71
Notepad 34
Novell Netware 85

O

Objectives, short-term 23
Online forms 58
Ownership 82

P

Page design 68
Paint Shop Pro 44
Paper, reducing 7, 128
Paper-based document 70
Paperless office 128